Cody McDevitt has brought to life a little recognized tragic episode in African American and Johnstown history. Recalling the national debate about race and constitutional rights and the willingness to express dictatorial rule over black lives by white elected officials was not just a scene in large urban areas, but the small mid-American heartland as well.
—Samuel W. Black, director, African American Program,
Senator John Heinz History Center

BANISHED
FROM JOHNSTOWN

Racist Backlash in Pennsylvania

CODY MCDEVITT
FOREWORD BY TONY NORMAN

THE
History
PRESS

Published by The History Press
Charleston, SC
www.historypress.com

Copyright © 2020 by Cody P. McDevitt
All rights reserved

Front cover design by Alisha Wormsley.

First published 2020

Manufactured in the United States

ISBN 9781467142748

Library of Congress Control Number: 2019951253

Comfort the Afflicted and Afflict the Comfortable

CONTENTS

CONTENTS

FOREWORD

Everyone knows about the Johnstown Flood of 1889, though no one alive today personally experienced that calamity in western Pennsylvania in real time.

Eminent historians have written about it. Poets have waxed eloquent about the destruction caused by the failure of the South Fork Dam that killed more than 2,200 people.

Best-selling sheet music was commissioned nearly a century before Bruce Springsteen sang about it on *Nebraska*. Plays were staged about its aftermath. One of the first silent movies memorialized it.

There's a well-regarded Flood Museum that has as its mission the preservation of every relevant detail of that deluge. For those who want to pay their respects, there's also the Johnstown Flood National Memorial, a solemn edifice that commemorates the 777 people whose bodies were recovered after the Conemaugh River's rampage but never identified.

Even those tempted to forget the city's history of flooding can't get around the 18 percent "Johnstown Tax" on liquor sales in Pennsylvania, which deposits $300 million annually into the state's general fund decades after the last puddle evaporated in the second flood.

That's why it would be inconceivable for anyone living in Johnstown today to be stumped by a question about one of the greatest natural disasters in American history. There's a monument or placard everywhere you look, lest one forget.

The average Johnstown resident's grasp of regional history gets a little shakier once the subject turns to a disaster in 1923 that defined the town for much of the country a mere thirty-four years after a flood of biblical proportions put the community on the map in the first place.

On September 7, 1923, Mayor Joseph Cauffiel ordered all blacks and Mexicans who had been in Johnstown for less than seven years to leave town. He gave these citizens and migrants who had done nothing to warrant exile from their homes and communities less than a day to conclude their affairs and leave town—or face crippling fines and months in jail.

Cauffiel issued the unconstitutional edict in response to the fatal shooting of two police officers and the critical wounding of four others when they attempted to arrest a black man in Rosedale, a black neighborhood in Johnstown.

Mayor Cauffiel, a notorious racist even by the standards of the day, had been known for the draconian sentences he imposed on blacks and Mexicans who came before him in his capacity as a magistrate in the notorious "Mayor's Courts" that were still operating in Pennsylvania at the time.

An estimated two thousand African Americans and Mexicans uprooted their lives and left Johnstown rather than challenge Cauffiel in court, given his propensity for ignoring the law. Cauffiel was not only a sanctimonious teetotaler but also an incorrigible ally of the Ku Klux Klan, though he insisted that his campaign to racially cleanse Johnstown was rooted in concern for the welfare of these minorities—not racial hatred.

The expulsion of Johnstown's black and Mexican population was arguably the most important thing that happened in that city in the twentieth century, yet it is an event that has fallen into the region's memory hole. Most people have never heard of it. It isn't taught in regional schools. Unlike the Johnstown Flood, a disaster etched indelibly upon the minds of people born and raised there decades later, the events of 1923 are a source of shame and embarrassment.

The moral complicity of the white citizens in Johnstown who did nothing while Mayor Cauffiel made a mockery of the constitutional rights of black citizens and Mexican migrants is obvious. Amnesia comes in handy when evading historical guilt.

But what happens when the story of Cauffiel's attempts to deal with the "Negro Problem" resurfaces with all of its inglorious details decades later? What happens when a dogged journalist at the *Somerset Daily American* resurrects a pitiable drama of American terrorism an entire region has managed to forget?

Banished from Johnstown: Racist Backlash in Pennsylvania is rooted in a series of articles journalist Cody McDevitt wrote for the *Somerset Daily American*. The articles shocked readers because there was little to no memory of events that happened as recently as ninety-six years ago. It was a challenge to Johnstown's memory of itself.

Because there is no widespread memory of the exile that took place there, only the most historically literate know of the national scorn that fell on the city as the result of Mayor Cauffiel's hateful antics.

There has been no conscientious wrestling with the legacy of injustice, to say nothing of an acknowledgement that a crime of major proportions was committed.

All people in the area know from looking around is that the region lacks the diversity that has strengthened and enriched other cities. Those who aren't inclined to dig too deep have only the vaguest notion as to why that is.

Banished from Johnstown, Cody McDevitt's detailed, rich chronicle of the events leading up to the expulsion of blacks and Mexicans from Johnstown, not only fills the gap with much-needed history and context but also lets the reader know how racial banishment affected Johnstown for decades to come.

It probably isn't an easy story for people from Johnstown to read now, but it is a fascinating and necessary narrative of both a regional and national event that deserves to be pulled from obscurity.

As a result of what Johnstown did, Stowe Township tried to go a similar route at the time but failed. South Bend, Indiana, ordered blacks to leave town, and up to 1,500 obeyed the mandate within twenty-four hours. It was not a trend that was able to catch on nationally, despite the existence of far too many so-called sundown cities across the American landscape.

McDevitt's taut and propulsive narrative of Cauffiel's disastrous policy of racial exile is heavily sourced thanks to the attention paid to it by regional and national media at the time. The fact that it was so widely covered makes the lack of memory of the event all the more curious.

Banished from Johnstown corrects the historical record and shows how Johnstown fit, if relatively briefly, into the sad pattern of racial cleansing rearing its head across the country in the early 1920s. Though it lacked the death toll and ferocity of Tulsa and Rosewood, it was a laboratory of systemic injustice that shocked the conscience of much of the country. It is understandable that most of those who live in the area today have either forgotten about or never knew of this painful chapter of Johnstown's history.

Cody McDevitt's necessary book will especially rattle those with roots in the region stretching back a century. Why wasn't this story passed down along with older lore about the Johnstown Flood? Where is the placard reminding residents about a mighty injustice that was done in Johnstown?

Until that placard comes along, *Banished from Johnstown* will have to serve as the only honest broker of Johnstown's haunted racial past. Pennsylvania, and the nation, owes a debt to the young journalist who has recovered this woefully neglected story from the ash heap of history.

—Tony Norman, columnist, *Pittsburgh Post-Gazette*, spring 2019

INTRODUCTION

I knew Johnstown and western Pennsylvania had a history of racism, but it always seemed as if it wasn't what you would see in the southern United States. That kind of intolerance was at a different level. And yet, when studying our history here, there are remarkable instances of it.

I was surprised when I found out what happened in Johnstown in 1923, when two thousand African Americans and Mexicans were forced from their homes. But it was also painfully familiar. Drive through parts of the state, and you'll see Confederate flags on trucks and outside homes. You'll hear about white supremacist militias. There's an underlying sense that this is a white working-class area and all others are not quite welcome.

In the 1920s, the Ku Klux Klan organized faster in the Johnstown area than anywhere else in the state. Housing discrimination has been a longtime issue for black families. And other instances of persecution happened. Recently, a man drove a pickup truck through a black neighborhood in Johnstown with a banner that said, "In loving memory of James Earl Ray," honoring the man who assassinated Martin Luther King Jr. He also had a black mannequin that hung over the tailgate on one side of the truck. Those people are in the minority here, but they are still part of the Johnstown community.

The story was forgotten by and large. But it' s still timely, and it always will be. There are always political figures attempting to exploit racial prejudices to advance their agenda. Though there are certainly sobering parts of this story, there are also inspiring accounts of journalists and activists forcing an injustice to end.

Whether you are an African American, a Mexican, another ethnicity or a white person, understanding that we have a history of committing crimes against the minorities of the country helps us realize that we must strive to do better. Our fates and rights are inextricably bound, as Dr. King once said. To threaten one group's rights means to threaten all groups' rights.

What the Johnstown mayor did was atrocious, but it isn't without precedent in the nation's history. Part of the goal of this book was to explain the things that he thought permitted him to do it. Those explanations are still given to justify wrongdoing. It is just as bad now as it was then.

Let us permit history to inform our understanding of contemporary events. The traits of certain historical figures manifest themselves repeatedly in future leaders. Knowing injustices from the past and what was done to resist them will help us uphold what is right.

SHOCK AND THE SEARCH FOR A CAUSE

Fear and uncertainty gripped most of Rosedale on the morning of September 7, 1923. What the black people there read in the paper was unlike anything they had ever seen, even in the Deep South. Mayor Joseph Cauffiel told the *Johnstown Democrat* he'd ordered all black and Mexican people who lived in town for less than seven years to leave the city, threatening to use the force of law to make sure his dictate was followed. How had it come to this? It couldn't have just been the shooting of the police officers. Why seven years? All of the residents in Rosedale, the black neighborhood in Johnstown, asked those questions among themselves.

Tension was in the air the past few years, but this mandate was unprecedented. Those being kicked out of town already knew Mayor Cauffiel to be vindictive, but some were determined to stay in the city, regardless of the order. Many, however, were afraid and made plans to leave before things got worse.

Johnstown was a city on edge in the 1920s. A lot of it had to do with the influx of different groups and ethnicities that poured into it during the decades following the Civil War. That combined with booming industry created a potential for civil unrest. Johnstown had a population of 67,327 in 1920, and by 1923, some estimates pegged it as high as 100,000. The first settlers were Welsh, followed by the Irish, then the Hungarians, Poles, Slavs, Czechs and Italians. After the war ended, African Americans and Mexicans settled in the area. In the social strata of Johnstown, Welsh, Irish, German, English, Scottish and Swedish immigrants were higher up

than the Poles, Slovenians, Croatians, Serbians, Slovaks, Slavs and Italians. Black people and Mexicans were at the very bottom. The quality of housing corresponded to that social strata, according to Ewa Morawska's essay "Johnstown's Ethnic Groups" in the local history book *Johnstown: Story of a Unique Valley*.

The Irish, Germans and Welsh founded the earliest ethnic social clubs and organizations. These groups assimilated into Johnstown and became the most powerful, well-established factions in the city. Jewish immigrants also came after fleeing persecution in Europe. They were predominantly peddlers and merchants. Jews were excluded from most jobs, including those in the steel mill.

The Cambria Iron Works, the primary steel mill in the city, became more successful as the decades progressed, and its need for unskilled labor increased. At the same time, a large number of immigrants from southern and eastern European countries began coming to the country. They wanted to save money to build a better life back in Europe. The men came alone before sending for their families. Only about a third of them went back to Europe. The rest remained in America. The immigrants faced prejudice and tough living situations. They were referred to as "Hunkies."

They mostly settled in Cambria City and Minersville, two neighborhoods in Johnstown. Living conditions were unsanitary, and infant mortality was high. From 1890 to 1910, the city's population of southern and eastern European immigrants grew from 2,400 to more than 12,000. The safest and highest-paying jobs went to native-born Americans first and then immigrants from Wales, Scandinavia, Ireland and Germany. Those from southern and eastern Europe were forced to take jobs with lower wages and worse working conditions. Work in a mill or mine was dangerous,

Johnstown was a booming mill town during the early part of the twentieth century. Here's a panoramic view of the Lower Works of the Cambria Iron Company, 1908. *Library of Congress, Prints and Photographs Division, Washington, D.C.*

especially for untrained employees, and many accidents occurred. The management grouped immigrants by nationality into crews so that they could communicate in their native languages. They also hoped to prevent them from organizing a union.

It is important to note how entrenched the black community was. African Americans had been in Johnstown since before the Civil War, when it was a central location for the Underground Railroad. A small settlement of African Americans was present on Laurel Mountain near Johnstown in 1825. The first area African American church began meeting in a log cabin as early as 1840. In 1854, many of Johnstown's black residents, led by the Reverend Samuel Williams, immigrated to Liberia.

But it wasn't until after the Civil War that their presence was really established. That's when a band of pioneers, including former slaves Charles W. Cook, William Roberts and Louis Rideout, came to work at the Woodvale Tannery—a brick building two and a half stories high that contained 230 vats and employed seventy-five men. The tannery shipped hides to Massachusetts to be used in manufacturing high-quality women's shoes. The leather produced at the facility won a number of prizes, including first place at the Vienna World's Fair.[1]

William Rosensteel, the owner of the tannery, went to Maryland to recruit labor. When the black people came, they found one African American family in Johnstown, headed by John Kelly. In what were the outskirts of the city, they found the families of Abram Blaine and Joseph Lindsay.

When he was nineteen, Cook had fought in the Civil War with the colored troops under the command of Union general Ambrose Burnside. Cook was in the Battle of the Weldon Railroad and in the Battle of Petersburg. Cook, a tall, slender and dignified man, lived to be ninety-one, conducting his life as one of the great statesmen within the African American community in Johnstown.

They worked long hours and settled in makeshift houses, but their success let them organize a church. After much difficulty finding a Zion minister, the congregation retained the services of the Reverend M.W. Knox of Hollidaysburg, about forty miles east of Johnstown. The church was in a school building. There were eight charter members, and it was named Cambria Chapel A.M.E. Zion Church.

In September 1875, the Reverend J.H. Baptist was appointed to lead the church. The schoolhouse no longer fit the congregation's needs, and the members secured a new location. They received a lot from the Cambria Iron Company. A year later, the railroad brought a group of black laborers to Johnstown. That group met each Sunday in different homes for religious service, and in a short time they founded the Mount Olive Baptist Church. For forty years, those two churches were the only black ones in town. They were the centers of activity for the black community.[2]

When the great Johnstown Flood happened in 1889, the black tannery workers lost all their possessions and their row homes, which were located along Gautier Street. Nearly all of them survived, however, and they moved to other sections of the city. As they came, they continued to fight for their place.[3]

The black population worked for equality in 1900, when it established the Afro-American Union League. Each summer, the community also celebrated Freedom Day, commemorating the Emancipation Proclamation, and Jerry Spriggs roasted an ox. Spriggs, a barber by trade and an ex-slave, cooked it for hours, usually at Roxbury Park.

Nelson Raynor, a white journalist, wrote about the growing black population in the city in 1903 for the *Johnstown Democrat*. He thought it was impossible for whites and blacks to coexist in the same area and quoted a black man in his article: "The colored man must remember his position and must not think he is better than the white man....His ancestors for centuries were slaves and he cannot catch up with the others," the source told Raynor. "He has a place of his own, and so long as he stays in his place and attends to his business he will succeed in his work."

In late September 1904, a white woman in Patton, which is near Johnstown, reported to authorities that a black man raped her for more than five hours near a railroad track. She frightened him off when she screamed. News of the deed spread like wildfire among the townspeople, and it aroused a mob spirit. Several hundred men scoured the countryside for an unidentified black man. A police officer secured a buggy to whisk away a suspect before the mob could lynch him. The man who was eventually arrested for the crime was later vindicated after the woman said he was not the one who had done it.

There were three recorded lynchings in Pennsylvania, but the number of attempted extralegal executions is unknown. Three years after the Johnstown lynching attempt, in Pittsburgh, a mob of several hundred chased after a black man following an altercation with a newsboy. Some African Americans fought back, but they soon became targets. The gang of white people hurled a number of racial epithets as well as stones and other objects. Cries of "lynch them" and "kill them" emanated from the hostile crowd. The lynching attempt ended when firemen and police officers dispersed the mob.

Dr. Michael J. Pfeifer, author of *Lynching Beyond Dixie: American Mob Violence Outside the South*, explained the phenomenon: "This sort of 'near lynching' prevented lynching in which a mob gathers but the lynching never comes off, because of effective preventative action by law enforcement, a lack of will on the part of the mob, etc., may have been the most common expression of the lynching impulse in northern states such as Pennsylvania, but have been understudied by scholars."

Tensions between Johnstown's black and white communities increased in 1916. That year, as part of the Great Migration, masses of black people arrived in Johnstown by every means of travel available to them. Word had gotten out that they could make a decent living there. They fled persecution and wanted to be closer to the American dream. The small city in western Pennsylvania was just one community they went to. Black southerners came to work in the mills and mines across the Midwest and in the Northeast.

Dr. Spencer Crew, who is a curator at the National Museum of African American History and Culture in Washington, D.C., said that new arrivals' experiences differed depending on the places they went to settle. Most moved to where they had connections. In the best instances, friends and family met them. In the worst, they were on their own.

"Those experiences varied over towns," Crew said. "So in Johnstown, it depended on who was coming and what connections they had. Usually they didn't go there blindly. Usually they sensed there was opportunity in that location for them."

The newcomers were perceived differently than those who had been there for a long time, according to Charles Lumpkins, a professor of labor and employment relations at Penn State University. "The established black populations, there was more of a preponderance of families who had been there for two or three generations," Lumpkins said. "They had northern ways. Their work habits were like Northerners. They had absorbed more Northern culture. Their churches were less animated than the stereotypical white or Southern worship services."

In the South, they had been treated as second-class citizens, and they frequently lived in residences that drew water from wells polluted with wastewater. Rental houses in the South often had no sinks. Lynching was a fact of life and perhaps the greatest reason for the mass movement. And the North had been portrayed as a land of opportunity. Johnstown's black population quadrupled between 1910 and 1920, going from 442 to 1,650.[4]

Ben Cashaw came from Georgia with his father and brothers. Years later, he told the *Johnstown Tribune-Democrat* why he left the South: "The economic system of the South had decayed," Cashaw said. "There was nothing to look forward to."

They were people like Joseph Davis, who came to Johnstown from a farm in Orange County, Virginia, where he had been the water boy on the farm. He traveled all over the nation before arriving in Johnstown. His father worked on the Baltimore and Ohio Railroad. Davis rode the rails to Johnstown, hopping between freight trains.

"Didn't you ever do that?" he later asked a reporter. "Everybody hoboed around the country then. If you didn't have any money, that's the way you traveled."[5]

He and a buddy hopped off a train in the Conemaugh Yards of the Pennsylvania Railroad and walked to the Crystal Hotel on Washington Street, where his brother was a porter. Davis got a job at the Capitol and later the Penn Traffic Company store on Washington Street. He was eventually hired at the Crystal Hotel as a bellhop. When he dressed too well, some whites forced Davis off the sidewalks or spat at him. And there were always the unpleasant names the whites used for black people.

Leroy Hemphill, of LaFayette, Georgia, told a historian about his father coming

Joseph Davis, who served in France with black troops under the command of General John "Black Jack" Pershing, who was white, as were all commanding officers. Davis was discharged in 1919. *Courtesy of the African-American Heritage Society in Johnstown.*

to Johnstown to get employment at Bethlehem. Leroy was three years old at the time. "I can remember the men putting coal on the train," he said in a documentary about local black history. "The main reason we came was economic. The boll weevil was king of the South at the time. And California had become the cotton capital of the world. Labor was at a low end and the times were too hard to make it."

Northern industrial leaders welcomed the African Americans. During World War I, the federal government restricted immigration from European countries, so businesses faced a labor shortage. Thus, black employees became more attractive.[6]

Identified as Mr. Wells of Prospect, in Johnstown, this man recruited African Americans in the South to come to the city to work at Bethlehem Steel. *Courtesy of the African-American Heritage Society in Johnstown.*

Agents from railroads, munitions factories and other defense industries facilitated the migration. Steel mill owners sent recruiters to the South to lure black labor north. Since most labor unions excluded black workers, iron and steel officials were anxious to hire them. Agents were both black and white men.

Jack Johnson, a black man in Johnstown who was once the servant of Cambria Steel general manager Charles Price, was a recruiter. Johnson was highly successful. Those whom he enrolled, about fifty each trip, were seated on railway coaches destined for Johnstown. The recruits were typically African American men without wives or family. His son Burrell Johnson told the *Johnstown Tribune-Democrat* years later about his travels. His father had come to the city from Winchester, Virginia, to work for Price, whose home was in Westmont, the traditionally well-to-do area in Johnstown.

"The company had problems during the war," Burrell said. "They needed laborers. So they sent my father to different places in the South to get workers. He went to towns in Alabama and Mississippi and would bring back black workers by the railroad-car load."

When Burrell's father went into the southern towns, he met the police first because he couldn't do anything until they agreed to let him. "They weren't too happy about losing their laborers because as long as they had a lot of laborers, they had cheap labor," Burrell said. "So I'm sure they took the opportunity to get rid of some of their bad workers. So we got our share of good and bad workers."

The steel company gave Johnson a bank draft of $1,000 to pay the railroad fare to Johnstown for the recruits, who later repaid the amount from their wages in the mill.

After they arrived, people gave the agents the names of relatives who might have been interested in coming. Another aid to the agents was the placement of newspaper ads for work up north in black newspapers.

When black people started arriving en masse in 1916, northern Democrats viewed them skeptically. In 1916, the *Johnstown Democrat* wrote about the colonization of black people in the buildup to that year's election. Agents from the U.S. Department of Justice came to investigate the newcomers. The agents had plain talks with people who were in touch with black recruits. They were prepared to safeguard the election. The *Johnstown Democrat* claimed that the Republican Party was planning on using floaters—newly arrived black migrants who would be willing to vote a certain way in exchange for money—in the next election. Black people who came north denied that they had been brought there for any other reasons aside from work.

Many of the white workers who were already in Johnstown opposed their importation. During Mayor Louis Franke's tenure from 1916 to 1920, representatives of organized white labor appealed to him to take action to prevent black people from coming. Franke told the unions to take it up with the steel companies. But he said he wouldn't let the city be filled with bad people. Steel companies told the representatives that they would exercise care in hiring men and that in no event would there be an effort to flood the community with black labor.[7]

"I don't think there is any area in the United States that was totally open to migrants whether it was people of color or Latinos or Asians," asserted Samuel W. Black, director of African American Programs at the Heinz History Center in Pittsburgh. "We haven't always been a welcoming society. You could say the same thing about Jews, Italians and other ethnicities."

Fifty thousand black people came into western Pennsylvania following World War I. When they arrived, they were usually placed in companies of two or three hundred in various steel mills in communities throughout the region or in railroad and construction camps. On average, they made forty to forty-eight cents an hour for a nine-to-ten-hour workday. The average pay in railroad camps was forty cents an hour, and construction camps were the highest paying at fifty cents an hour. That's around six dollars an hour in today's value.

The mills primarily put them in unskilled positions. But they made significantly more money than they had on southern farms. The higher cost of living was offset because the average income was 70 percent higher. Discrimination locked many in lower positions, however. White foremen at the steel mills frequently fired black workers and replaced them with people of their own ethnicity.

Unlike African Americans who came to the region before the Great War, the new generation of black steelworkers didn't experience much upward mobility and didn't gain many of the bigger positions in the mills. Most of the big-time posts in the Johnstown mills belonged to native white workers or European immigrants. The late arrival of many of those workers subjected them to discrimination.

In 1920, African Americans accounted for 10.9 percent of the steel mill labor force in Pennsylvania. Their importance grew with each passing year. African Americans in Johnstown sent letters and money south to encourage migration. Dr. W.T.B Williams, a black investigator at the time, remarked on a U.S. Department of Labor study that described the movement. "The unusual amounts of money coming in, the glowing accounts from the North, and the excitement and stir of great crowds leaving, work upon the feelings of many Negroes," Williams said. "They pull up and follow almost without a reason. They are stampeded into action. This accounts in large part for the apparently unreasonable doings of many who give up good positions or sacrifice valuable property or good businesses to go north."

A second period of enormous growth in the local black community came in 1922 and culminated the next year. The black population of Johnstown was estimated to be between 1,500 and 3,000 by 1923. They were scattered in four different districts. One of them was across from the Conemaugh River and in the rear of Napoleon Street, where they were exceedingly well spoken of by white residents, and they had their own homes.

The African Americans who came to the city following the war primarily settled in Rosedale, along with a collection of Mexican immigrants, who arrived in large numbers as well.

Mexicans in Pennsylvania found employment in the steel mills. They sent money back to Texas or Mexico to bring relatives to the area. One man came from Texas and convinced seven brothers and three sisters, together with their families, to come to Johnstown. The steel companies employed practically all the Mexicans as laborers. A few were semiskilled, and others were trained as mechanics, according to an academic treatise written by Paul S. Taylor titled *Mexican Labor in the United States, Bethlehem, Pennsylvania*. There were artisans among them and carpenters and machinists, but they were not asked to do those crafts because they didn't speak English. One steel executive thought that Mexican workers were better than black employees.

Some executives felt that Mexican labor was better than European labor.

"The main thing in handling Mexicans is patience," one executive said. "How would you feel if you were a young, non-English-speaking Mexican about 27 years old, who had never seen a piece of machinery, and were suddenly to obtain a job here? It takes the native of Mexico quite a time to get used to the idea that he must arrive at a certain time and remain on the job all day long."

The federal and state governments seemed anxious to have a considerable labor supply from Mexico. Employers and businessmen who dealt with them in Johnstown told newspapers that many of the Mexican newcomers were industrious, honest and ambitious. But many others in the community regarded them as unproductive criminals.

Mexicans came so they could escape the constraints of poverty, which at the time devastated their native country. Between 1900 and 1930, one-tenth of Mexico's population came to the United States. The political controversy over their arrival reached an apex in the 1920s. The Mexican Revolution, which took place between 1910 and 1920, drove many Latinos to flee the country's violence.

In June 1916, the *Johnstown Tribune* featured an article about local Mexicans. In it, the men interviewed described the starvation, oppression and warlike conditions back home.

At first, their employment was primarily in the southwestern United States, but eventually northern industrial centers recruited them to work there. By the 1920s, they appeared in meatpacking plants, automobile factories and railroads throughout the Midwest. The influx made local people think about the nature of the newcomers. They were often compared unfavorably with the white majority of the nation as well as the immigrants coming from Europe. Many viewed them as indigenous peons whose traits were racially determined. Though many who worked with Mexican immigrants thought differently, the larger American public thought they were lazy and backward.

Industrialists thought Mexicans were easily manipulated and thus were good people to work in their facilities. Protestant ministers and missionaries tried to convert the Mexican population, as many were devout Catholics. Andrew Sandoval-Strausz, director of the Latino studies program at Penn State University, said that a racist and racialist way of thinking was ascendant in 1923. "They were worried that the country's character was going to be fundamentally changed," he asserted.

Groups such as the Ku Klux Klan thought Mexicans hurt America. And so the newcomers were persecuted much like other minorities. Many Klan members pushed for restrictive policies regarding Mexican immigration. When Congress passed the 1921 Immigration Act and then a few years later supported the passage of the National Origins Act, representatives acknowledged that they should limit the total number of immigrants coming into the country and take into account biological heritage and race.

White workers' fear of losing their jobs to Mexicans existed long ago. It's been a typical reaction to that ethnicity in this country. The Reverend Colin Bossen, who wrote a doctoral dissertation at Harvard University about racial relations during that era, said that the bigotry of today has roots in what happened in the 1920s and even further in the past.

"I think we start to see that it is this very long tradition of continuity. It's a pathology that stretches back deep into American history," Bossen said. "It's not a foreign phenomenon. You have people on the left who describe people on the right as fascists and exoticizing them. But in fact white supremacy is deeply rooted in American history. One thing that we get from studying this early history is understanding how deep this pathology goes. And then we realize how much we have to grapple with it. It's not something that is now coming into vogue. It's been a part of the American landscape for generations."

Whites thought mill owners pulled down white labor with their support and importation of black labor. So the white workers made African Americans feel unwelcome. Even if blacks wanted to join local labor unions, the organizations' leaders often excluded or treated them in a hostile manner. And employers frowned upon union participation, which also made black people less eager to join.

"They were surprised by the way they were treated," said Dr. Ralph Proctor, who teaches ethnic and diversity studies at the Community College of Allegheny County. "They had been told that if you got north that racism wouldn't exist. But they found out it existed strongly. It was a little more subtle than the South, but it was just as bad. The South had Jim Crow laws, and the North had Jim Crow customs that operated the same way."

The *Johnstown Democrat* editorialized about the issue in a racist way in a December 1919 column called "Mixing the Labor Problem":

> *The practical question arises as to whether a southern darkey is not really an alien, when he is brought north and plumped down in the midst of one*

of our northern industrial communities....Alien is as alien does and thinks. The southern darkey's point of view, his manner of living, his customs and practices, are most assuredly not those of the north. Negro labor from the south, many think, does not make a desirable addition to community life. Since we have the problems of the alien pressing so strongly, at least as far as a great many of our well-meaning patriots are concerned, would it not be just as well to refrain from complicating them by adding the southern darkey to the northern melting pot?

The article's author also criticized the effort to import Mexican labor:

In addition to the southern darkey, who is an alien with respect to the north, there is indeed the menace of the Mexican. This menace is not confined to the land south of the Rio Grande. It is much nearer home than that. There are a number of industrial concerns in this country that, at the present time, are angling for Mexican workers. If the Mexican is a bad man; if he is a troublemaker; if he is untrustworthy, and treacherous, why snatch him from his native environment and make a neighbor of him? It is not enough to answer that the Mexican is cheap labor, for cheap labor has ceased to be a consideration in this country.

At the time, the diplomatic relationship between Mexico and the United States was deteriorating. Some clamored for war. The newspaper speculated that the desire for lower wages might have something to do with an industrial push for more workers. The editorial continued:

The fact that American industry is fishing for Mexican labor reveals a new angle to the intervention proposition. If we were to conquer Mexico, doubtless we could round up Mexicans and ship them to our industrial captains by the trainload. The employer who needed help might be able to convince himself that Mexicans were 100 percent American. One wonders whether the growing predilection for Mexican labor evinced in some quarters not so very far away, has anything to do with the demand that we proceed to knock Mexico into a cocked hat.

Nearly one thousand Mexicans came to South Bethlehem, Pennsylvania, between April 6 and May 30, 1923. They proceeded to go elsewhere, with Johnstown among the places they went. Employment agencies recruited Mexicans in San Antonio, Texas, and sent them northward on special trains at a cost to be repaid out of future wages.[8] A large number of Mexicans who came to Johnstown also came from the El Paso district. The importation of Mexican labor in that manner became widespread in the steel industry.

In July 1923, the *Marshall News Messenger* in Texas reported that many Mexican laborers had passed through town in the previous few months to take jobs in the coal mines and steel mills of the North and East. One morning, a special train of nine cars with 365 laborers onboard was en route to Johnstown, where they would go to work.

There was tumult that came along with the newcomers. When a journalist from the *Philadelphia North American* came to town in 1919, he said the city was at a tipping point because of its treatment of labor. The article started with a comparison of Johnstown and nearby Altoona, saying that "while Altoona is solving its after-the-war reconstruction problems on broad-minded American principles, the Chamber of Commerce and the Central Labor Union, working hand-in-hand against the upper autocrats and nether Bolshevists, stupid Johnstown Bourbonism is still dancing in its rose gardens surrounded by seething volcanoes of industrial discontent and unrest."

He described the city as strutting with wealth, with big new hotels, banks, stores and affluence sprawling and loitering everywhere while poorer people struggled to make it. The environment was ripe for exploitative people. Sandoval-Strausz noted those factors created a combustible situation in Johnstown and elsewhere. "There is a sense that these people bring dangerous ideas into the U.S.," he said. "Between all those things, the basic fact was that humans view race as determining who you are. They're used to these racist terms of brutes and brute characteristics to describe them. They apply that to Mexicans."

The steel industries in Johnstown were those principally owned by the Bethlehem Steel Company, which some time before acquired them from the Midvale Steel and Ordnance Company. Bethlehem Steel's finished products included steel freight cars, wheels and axles; wire and wire products; rolled steel blanks for gears, flywheels and circular forgings; bars; steel mine ties; steel plates; ingots; blooms; billets; bands; and slabs.

The presence of the Bethlehem mill led to a number of other businesses, including welding, furniture sales and production, bakeries and butchers. The central business district in downtown Johnstown was the hub of its commerce, entertainment and transportation. With one exception in East Conemaugh, all the banks were headquartered there. Almost all lawyers, insurance agencies, real estate firms, engineers and accountants had offices in that area.

The south front of the Penn Traffic Building along Washington Street. Johnstown was a booming town with several department stores, including this one. *Library of Congress, Prints and Photographs Division, Washington, D.C.*

Johnstown housed every major department store except John Widmann and Sons. The largest store was the Penn Traffic Company, which occupied 250,000 square feet of retail space and had about five hundred employees. It was the largest store in Pennsylvania outside of Pittsburgh and Philadelphia. The best restaurants were in the downtown area, but black people were not allowed to sit at their counters or their tables.

There were two primary newspapers in town: the *Johnstown Tribune* and the *Johnstown Democrat*. Anderson Walters, a powerful figure in Republican politics at the time, owned and published the *Tribune*. The newspaper reflected his political inclinations. He featured international news, usually on the front page, with a local section showcasing regional developments. Walters was generally progressive in his attitudes regarding race, ethnicity and civil rights. In 1902, when he bought the newspaper, the editors and reporters stopped using words like "Pollack," "Hun" or "Slav" to describe eastern European immigrants. He favored building more playgrounds in the city to keep youths occupied. He was a Prohibition supporter.

The *Tribune*'s rival newspaper was the *Johnstown Democrat*, which was owned by Warren Worth Bailey, a leader in the Democratic Party. Both

Above: The Penn Traffic Store in Johnstown was one of a few large department stores in a booming town that grew larger every year. Immigrants poured in from Europe to work in its steel mill industry and coal mining sector. Migrants from the South and from Mexico were also recruited to work there. *Courtesy of the Johnstown Area Heritage Association.*

Right: Anderson Walters, owner of the *Johnstown Tribune*, was the city's leading Republican voice. Walters and Warren Worth Bailey, owner of the rival *Johnstown Democrat*, were often at odds over policy at the city, state and federal levels. Both had pursued political careers. *Library of Congress, Prints and Photographs Division, Washington, D.C.*

newspapers frequently carried news of the other publisher's foibles and failures of leadership. Bailey was the leader of the Democratic Party in Johnstown and Cambria County and the principal owner and publisher of the *Democrat*. Bailey served in Congress for two terms, from 1913 to 1917. Bailey was one of the leading Democrats in Pennsylvania. Prior to moving to Johnstown, he was an editorial writer for the *Chicago News* and the *Chicago Evening Mail*. When he came to Johnstown in 1893, he soon acquired the *Democrat*, which he and his brother Homer Bailey conducted for many years. Bailey expressed himself as a foe of the Ku Klux Klan, which hated him. George Wertz, a former sheriff and state senator, owned a third newspaper, the *Johnstown Daily Leader*.

There were two downtown theaters in Johnstown, both of which were unavailable to black people. The Cambria Theater was on Main Street near Market. The Johnstown Opera House accommodated 1,700 people, and it was located on Franklin and Locust Streets. Both places brought in traveling actors, vaudevillians, magicians, acrobats, musicians and lecturers who went from city to city providing professional entertainment during that time. William Jennings Bryan spoke there.

The city was a mixture of Republicans and Democrats. Elections went both ways in Johnstown, but the Republican Party dominated Johnstown for most of the 1920s. The party included people of all religions and races. Though it had people who supported legalizing alcohol, it was by and large the party for the dry forces. Thus it received overwhelming support from religious organizations that supported the temperance movement. In Johnstown, from 1918 to 1923, there were mixed opinions regarding booze. Some thought it was a shame that people couldn't get a drink legally, while others said the lawlessness that people undertook to get it was the bigger issue and the one that needed to be addressed. Prohibition enforcement and violations were central to most of the problems that city leaders faced.

In the 1910s, there was an effort to "Americanize" immigrants who came to Johnstown. Much like elsewhere, they insisted everyone speak the same language and observe the same customs. One of the effects was that it brought immigrants together, regardless of nationality. They knew they faced the same challenge. There was a lot of ethnic bashing among people who were part of what was known as Old Johnstown, which was composed of people whose ancestors there went back to its earliest days. They stereotyped the newcomers. Newspapers in town highlighted criminal tendencies within various ethnicities, particularly black people and Mexicans. Journalists frequently described them as hordes.

Warren Worth Bailey was the owner of the *Johnstown Democrat*, which was the publication advancing and advocating for the Democratic Party in Cambria County. Bailey was an opponent of Joseph Cauffiel throughout most of his career. *Library of Congress, Prints and Photographs Division, Washington, D.C.*

Regardless of the racism encountered in Johnstown, African Americans and Mexicans continued to come. In July 1923, the Pennsylvania Department of Labor reported that there was a shortage of workers in Johnstown. Five thousand men were needed for rough lines of work. Economic experts felt an influx of black laborers from the South would relieve the labor shortage.

In Johnstown, the black and Mexican communities were inextricably bound. They lived in the same quarters and neighborhoods such as Rosedale, which was about three miles north of the business district of the city of Johnstown. The coke ovens for Bethlehem were located there. To reach it, a person had to travel through the Minersville section of town, then over a rough road on the hillside through the country to the settlement. Before the building of the steel plant, it was considered a beautiful and delightful valley and residential area.

The steel executives purchased the nearby homes, and all the property eventually belonged to Bethlehem. With the closing of the valley road and the building of the road on the hillside, the lower portion of Rosedale was placed in a pocket with a high hill to the west and with filings from the mill on the south and east to a height of about seventy-five feet. Farther up the valley, the other portion of the settlement locally designated as Upper Rosedale was the wider part. There were approximately twenty-five houses in Lower Rosedale and two camps, or sets of bunkhouses, where Mexicans were quartered. Black people ran the boardinghouses.[9]

Though some remained optimistic about their lives, their housing conditions were deplorable. When Dean Kelly Miller of Howard University's Junior College visited in 1923, he said he had never seen worse living situations: "I have visited all types and kinds of communities in which Negroes live in all parts of the United States....I have seen them in alleys and shady places; I have witnessed their poverty and distress in city and country. But I can truthfully say that it has never been my good fortune or misfortune to look upon such pitiable conditions as prevailed in Johnstown."

Miller reported that only two black families owned homes. He said it was not due to their indolence—rather, they had faced restrictions and limitations in real estate transactions. Miller visited a stockade with one hundred residents. The sheets and pillowcases, judging from appearance, hadn't been changed for months. Smoke, dirt and grease was an inch thick on the floor.

"My soul sank within me as I saw splendid specimens of physical young manhood, fresh from the open air of the South, immersed in this dreadful environment, destructive alike to body and soul," Miller wrote.

The valley in which the Rosedale work camps were located. The coke works was a few miles down the road from this part of the community. *Photo by the author.*

Miller visited a shanty in one of the remote hollows with a single lamp without a chimney, whose dense smoke stifled the air. Someone drove Miller through the red-light district, which he said was too loathsome to describe.

"Human life is simply impossible in such an environment as this," Miller wrote.

The bunkhouses were small shacks that had ventilation chiefly through the chinks in the walls. They were stuffy in summer, cold during the winter and just large enough to hold the bunks built against the walls. Men who worked different shifts at the mills and mines shared the same beds. Sanitation was primitive, and areas soon became hotbeds of germs. When the flu broke out, the men died with machine-gun rapidity. Those who came from the South suffered greatly because of the change of climate and different conditions of employment. They were highly susceptible to pneumonia, tuberculosis and other ills. And when black people got sick, doctors refused to treat them.

In western Pennsylvania, because of the unsanitary living conditions, African Americans died much younger. In Pittsburgh, whites usually passed away when they reached their seventies. For blacks, the life expectancy was in the thirties. Pneumonia was one reason, as was influenza, which spread more rapidly in cramped quarters, according to Dennis Dickerson's *Out of the Crucible: Black Steel Workers in Western Pennsylvania.*

Jack Johnson took matters into his own hands while seeing people die of those illnesses. Johnson took a trip to Washington, D.C., and went to Howard University, an all-black school, where he asked if a doctor was available to practice in Johnstown. He recruited Dr. Moses Clayborne, a warm-hearted, dedicated man who thrived on making himself available day and night. Clayborne's example inspired many other African Americans to become community leaders throughout the decades he was in the community.

Some black people who came to the city never intended to remain there, and they left when employment became scarce. Turnover was high among northern mills and industries. Black people who came to Rosedale had fewer places of amusement, and they often found entertainment in drinking, sex and gambling. "When a set of men gamble among themselves, one man's loss is supposed to be another man's gain," Miller wrote. "But in Johnstown all the men are broke and no one seems any better off after the game is over."

Within the sordid atmosphere in Johnstown, the Reverend W. Sloan organized the Mount Sinai Baptist Church in 1917. It began as a bunkhouse, and later the flock worshipped in a company building shared with the Methodist group. After World War I ended, the bunkhouse was destroyed. But the church continued to grow with another building.[10]

Under the leadership of the Reverend J.H. Flagg, the group of Methodist families that settled in Rosedale organized the Bethel A.M.E. Church in 1917. He was emblematic of the working-class preachers who started churches up north during the Great Migration. His son Jesse Flagg remembered the early years of the church.

Left: Dr. Moses Clayborne, a physician who cared for the black community in Johnstown for decades. Clayborne was recruited to the city in the early years of the Great Migration because white doctors didn't treat black people. Clayborne was a beloved figure during his career because of his dignified leadership within the local African American population. *Courtesy of the Clayborne family.*

Right: J.H. Flagg came to Johnstown in 1916 after his blacksmith shop in Alabama burned down. He worked in the mills for thirteen cents an hour. He founded the Bethel A.M.E. Church in Rosedale, where black migrants settled when they came from the South. Flagg was emblematic of the working-class preachers who started churches up North during the Great Migration. *Courtesy of the Flagg family.*

"My family came here in 1916 when I was 11," he said to the *Tribune-Democrat* in 1980. "My father was a blacksmith in Enterprise, Alabama, but his shop burned down. So did our home and then the boll weevils flatted us out. So my father and my brother came here first and went to work for Cambria Steel Co. for 13 cents an hour. They got paid in gold pieces."

They held the first meeting of the Bethel A.M.E. Church in J.H. Flagg's daughter's home. A year later, parishioners established another branch in Conemaugh under the leadership of the Reverend L.A. Moore. Bethel A.M.E. was one of the churches the mill owners and executives supported.

"Employers supported black churches and black clergy because they expected them to inculcate sobriety and reliability in the laborers," said

Dickerson, a historian who has written extensively about local and regional black history. He continued,

> *These values, they hoped, would reduce turnover and develop community ties to Johnstown. Moreover, blacks whom employers engaged to do welfare work, whether in ministry, medicine, labor recruitment or social and recreational activities, were charged with the construction of community structures that would attract and retain blacks as permanent Johnstown residents and workers. The racism that surfaced in the 1920s that drove out some segment of the black population frustrated these efforts.*

Black people from Johnstown and across the country contributed to the country's efforts in World War I. African Americans in Johnstown who were drafted were given a royal send-off when they left for Camp Lee in Virginia. They left in good spirits after they were feted at a banquet. In a terrific downpour, the young men marched to the Fort Stanwix Hotel. Judge F.J.

The mortgage is burned at the Bethel A.M.E. Church in Johnstown later in its existence. J.H. Flagg organized the church in 1917. The first meeting was held in the home of his daughter. His congregation shared a building with the Mount Sinai Baptist Church. Previously, a white congregation had occupied it. *Courtesy of the church's congregation.*

O'Connor was the toastmaster. Mayor Louis Franke was among the guests of honor. The Reverend P.H. Williams, new pastor of the A.M.E. Zion Church, was the first speaker. He told the young men that they should feel proud that they had been selected to take a place in the army. He told them to be true to country and to themselves.

"And when you come back," said the minister, "democracy will rule the world. Feel like the soldier did back in the Civil War, who when his general said he wanted a flag planted on a fort replied, 'We'll plant that flag on that fort, General, or we'll report to God the reason why.' Now I want you to place old glory where it will hit the Kaiser hardest or report to God the reason why."

Attorney T.H.A. Moore, a civil rights leader in the community, noted that many people had expressed the hope that no one would go overseas. "Well, I hope you boys go over," Moore said. "I wouldn't want it written in history that there was a fight going on for democracy on the other side of the Atlantic and you colored boys had to stay over here and out of it."

The Reverend J.W. Coleman told them to be true to their country and to their race by being good, dutiful soldiers. The banquet closed with the singing of "The Battle Hymn of the Republic," which was led by the Reverend Williams. The *Johnstown Tribune* said the black soldiers deserved the same praise and support that their white counterparts received during the war:

> *The colored men who are today answering the call for their services with the Army, their families and friends and the community generally feel gratified that the departure of these soldiers is accompanied by precisely the same generous "send-off" that was given the white soldiers.*
>
> *The colored boys will serve the same flag and will face the same trials and dangers as the white troops. The committee in charge of the "send-off" ceremonies and dinner, the Fort Stanwix Hotel, and the members of the Local Board are to be congratulated for the breadth of vision and non-discriminating patriotism, which gives Johnstown's colored soldiers the same fine recognition which was tendered the white soldiers.*

The end of the war brought its own problems. When the soldiers returned home, local leaders worked to ensure they had jobs at mills and elsewhere. An article in the *Johnstown Democrat* relayed the story of a young Italian soldier who was without work and without resources: "I have no money and I will not beg," he was quoted as saying. "I will do any honest work."

The employment agent said that he hoped employers would get in the habit of hiring ex-soldiers. "If they would, we would be able to do justice to many of the servicemen who apply to us," agents commented to the newspaper in a company statement.

Mill owners still saw black and Mexican labor as cheaper and less likely to organize. So employers sometimes thought these minorities were better hires than some of the returning veterans or other immigrant groups. Hostility increased with these hiring trends. With so much going on, the city waited for some sort of civil strife. There was the possibility of revolution, fear of upheaval and the threat of dispossession.

While tension built in the city, union members pushed for higher wages and safer workplaces. Women pushed for suffrage, and black people pushed for an end to racism and for economic and political equality. Widespread unrest erupted in the strike of 1919 with all those forces at play.

"There were several perceptions going on. Everyone agreed that black Southerners came north for jobs during and after World War I," Lumpkins noted. "How they procured the jobs was split. Some thought they were strikebreakers. Some though they would take lower wages.

"A few people went beyond that and said they needed labor because immigration from Europe had stopped. Where would they turn to? The South again. Some people realized that it was a double-edged sword. Employers would love immigrants because it keeps down wages. But employees realized they could have higher wages with less employees. I'm sure that was the case in Johnstown."

Virtually the entire labor force of Johnstown honored the strike call on September 22, 1919. But by that November, the steel strike had become similar to others, and the steel companies rallied the community against the striking workers by gathering allies in the police, clergy and press. Pennsylvania governor William Sproul broke the strike when he sent in state troopers to maintain law and order. Though African Americans and Mexicans were often seen as strikebreakers in northern industrial centers, Johnstown's industries were reluctant to use them that way when the Great Steel Strike of 1919 took place.

In 1918, the Johnstown board of school directors created a special school for black children in Rosedale Borough. Two African American teachers instructed the students. About 110 black children enrolled in a school, which defied the statutes in Pennsylvania banning segregation in public schools. Though the prevailing understanding is that segregation was primarily a problem in the South, schools throughout the northern United States had separate school systems for black and white children well into the twentieth century. The Pennsylvania legislature enacted anti-segregation legislation in 1881. Though the law eliminated segregation in writing, it didn't get rid of it in practice.

Jesse Flagg, the preacher's son, told the *Tribune-Democrat* in 1980 about the school system in Rosedale. Black people who came from Alabama and Mississippi had a deep mistrust of white people because of the terrible experiences they had in the South. Many feared to associate with white people, particularly in schools. They had come from a segregated school system in the South. And many of them supported such a school system in Johnstown.

"In the South, we couldn't even send our children out to work with the whites," Flagg said. "We had to have an older black person there to see the children weren't taken advantage of."

Rosedale wasn't the only school African Americans went to in Johnstown prior to the 1920s. In most other schools in the city, black and white children attended class together. Charles Edgar Fairfax was the first black graduate of Johnstown High School in 1916. But the Rosedale School was unique in that it violated the state statute with support from both the white and black communities in Johnstown. Mr. W.E. Cephas was listed as the principal. In 1919, the board of directors appointed Ernest Swanston, a graduate of Howard University, as the new head of the school. Swanston married the granddaughter of the pastor of Shiloh Baptist Church. Swanston, a skilled pianist, taught piano lessons to public school students in the church. The Rosedale School and the two African American churches in the community worked closely together to educate children in the community.[11]

Some reflected on the early years of the settlement in a special section of the *Tribune-Democrat* that ran in 1980. The unidentified wife of James Whitehead was interviewed in 1980 about her experience in Rosedale. She had come from Clayton, Alabama, and recalled attending classes in the two-room schoolhouse in Rosedale. "Rosedale in those days was a peaceful valley between the hills west of Johnstown," she said. "We lived in old row company houses that weren't torn down until about 1947. There must have been 30 or 40 black families in Rosedale."

Many residents of Rosedale complained about the misrepresentation that steel company agents gave them about life in the North. They claimed they would have brick houses and a pay rate of sixty cents an hour in Johnstown. They had also been led to believe they would be permitted to attend dances with white people and share theaters and trains.

The Rosedale School in Johnstown was an all-black facility. Parents in both the white and black communities wanted segregation, which was in violation of Pennsylvania law. Still, segregation prevailed, aided by the wishes of both populations in Johnstown, in the early part of the century. Many other towns in the North also had segregated school systems well into the 1950s. *Courtesy of the African-American Heritage Society in Johnstown.*

Above: Ernest Swanston and his music class at Trinity Methodist Church in the 1940s. *Courtesy of the African-American Heritage Society in Johnstown.*

Opposite: A high view of the Rosedale Coke Plant, the primary industry in the black neighborhood of Johnstown. African Americans who lived in the community worked there as well as at other mills in the community. They were often tasked with the hardest and most dangerous jobs because their well-being was generally not considered as important as that of their white counterparts. *Courtesy of the Johnstown Area Heritage Association.*

Because of the growth in industry, the increased demand for homes required civic and industrial leaders to emphasize speed of construction rather than quality. The Johnstown area was crowded into a space surrounded by hills that didn't permit much expansion. In many cases, two houses were built on plots of ground where one was suitable.

Workplace hazards posed another threat. Steel mills usually clustered black workers in areas that white workers didn't tolerate. They often died or got injured at a much faster rate because of it. Supervisors assigned them to the galvanizing department, where zinc was used to coat wrought-iron pipes to prevent corrosion. Undertaking work in that area was detrimental to people's health as well because of the exposure to air pollutants.

Aside from the mills, the only other jobs available were those as bellhops, porters, maids, servants, chauffeurs and kitchen help. Many were barbers before Italians migrated to the area and took those positions. But mainly the jobs available were those in the open hearth, blast furnaces, sintering plant and coke plants. These positions were known as black men's jobs.

"People had the mistaken notion that because blacks came from the South, they could stand the heat better," steelworker Bill Cashaw told the *Tribune-Democrat* years later. "But we're human beings and it was just as hard on us as anybody else."

Racial discrimination happened outside the workplace as well. Throughout western Pennsylvania, public facilities didn't admit or serve black citizens. There were restrictions on where black people could sit in theaters, usually on the balcony. No swimming pools, public or private, were open to black people in Johnstown. They had to find places along out-of-the-way creeks and streams, which were often unsafe.

Churches and fraternal organizations provided safe havens from the persecution and helped newcomers acclimate. Much of Johnstown's black population worshipped at Cambria Chapel A.M.E. Zion Church and Mt. Olive Baptist Church. The churches were places of social upward mobility for black people who were being denied that movement in the larger white society. They took considerable pride in the increased status they earned as members, officers and preachers. Revivals were popular at the churches. People in attendance were thrilled to hear soul-stirring sermons or uplifting gospel music. The revivals served as recruiting drives. The churches were important for women, who found fellowship and upward mobility in them as much as the black men who came.

Fraternal organizations and black lodges grew enormously in the North during the Great Migration. Masonic and Elk Lodges were located throughout western Pennsylvania, including in Johnstown. Athletic organizations were also important in the region. Conemaugh Valley Lodge 10, Free and Accepted Masons, which was associated with the Prince Hall Affiliation, started in 1914. The Flood City Lodge 371, an Elks group with predominantly black membership, began in the 1920s.

Because black people were not allowed in white bars, they formed the Coachmen and Porter's Club. It was at Clinton and Locust Streets on the second floor. The men came for a few drinks, and on Saturday nights, they took women to dance there. Black women started the Elizabeth Lindsay Davis Club of Johnstown in May 1904. They formed the club after Lena Harris went to the organizational meetings in Pittsburgh and came back to start the club. The group used proceeds it raised to purchase coal for families, to help organizations and to aid college students. There was also a Woman's Christian Temperance Union for black women.

Quite a number of young black men met one night at the Cambria Chapel of the A.M.E. Church for the purpose of organizing a Young Men's Christian Association. The main YMCA in town was closed to black men. The Reverend P.H. Williams, who had been instrumental in furthering the movement, spoke on the necessity of the YMCA's work. The basement of the Cambria Chapel was to be used as the home of the newly formed organization until permanent quarters were secured. The plan didn't pan out, and the organization never took off.

The primary organization for the fight against discrimination in western Pennsylvania remained the National Association for the Advancement of Colored People. An NAACP branch was founded in the community in 1917. James Weldon Johnson, the first African American executive secretary of the national organization, visited the city in 1918 at the First Cambria A.M.E. Zion Church. The first article about the organization in the *Johnstown Tribune* said the NAACP's purpose was to "uplift the colored men and women of this country by securing to them the full enjoyment of their rights as citizens, justice in all courts and equality of opportunity everywhere. It favors and aims to aid every kind of education among them save that which teaches special privilege or prerogatives, class or caste. It recognizes the national character of the Negro problem and no sectionalism."

The organization said in a statement to the newspaper that its members abhorred crime and drew attention to the conditions that bred it. The article

Children play in Rosedale, the black and Mexican neighborhood in Johnstown, after a day in school. The community grew exponentially from 1917 until 1923, which was the beginning of the Great Migration, the name given to the mass movement of African Americans from the South to northern industrial centers. *Courtesy of the Johnstown Area Heritage Association.*

stated that the NAACP condemned mobs and people who took the law into their own hands in relation to black people accused of crimes:

> [The NAACP] *believes that the scientific truth of the Negro problem must be available before the country can see its way wholly clear to right existing wrongs. It has no other belief than that the best way to uplift the colored man is the best way to aid the white man to peace and social content: it has no other desire than exact justice and no other motive than humanity.*

T.H.A. Moore was the president of the Johnstown branch.

In the years following the war, there was a push both locally and nationally for equality. America had fought against intolerance overseas, yet it remained a part of everyday life for many of the country's minority citizens. Speakers arguing for civil rights came through Johnstown during that time, including William Monroe Trotter, executive secretary of the National Equal Rights League, in December 1919. Trotter was known mostly for being one of the first major challengers to Booker T. Washington's leadership in the African American community. He helped form the NAACP, though he refused to join the association's leadership. He founded and edited the *Boston Guardian*. Trotter told an audience at the Johnstown High School auditorium about his trip to a peace conference in Paris following World War I and spoke of the birth of the movement to secure equal rights for his race. Trotter had to take a position as a second cook on a small steamer bound for France to get there. The U.S. State Department told him that it wouldn't issue a passport, but it didn't cause him any problem.

"In Paris, there was no question of race or color—everyone had an equal right to restaurant and hotel accommodation—so I secured a room for the night," he told the audience.

WILLIAM MONROE TROTTER.

William Monroe Trotter, a prominent speaker at the time, came to Johnstown early on in the Great Migration to discuss his views on racial injustice and progress. Photo originally appeared in Boston City Council, *Exercises at the Dedication of the Statue of Wendell Phillips, July 5, 1915* (Boston: City of Boston, 1915), 11.

His goal during the peace conference was to bring the outrages that his race had suffered to the attention of President Woodrow Wilson and other delegates—he let them know that they needed democracy because of lynching, including of black women. He told them southern prejudice crept into northern states. He said, in part,

> *Now the Equal Rights League is officially represented in the League of Nations, we were permitted to present our amendment. The United States government has secured all the documents which I presented in Paris, and has had them printed in an official document. In that document is printed our case. Even if we have not received justice, the people of the world can never say that when a readjustment of the world was taking place—when democracy was being dispensed to all—that we did not present our case. We want liberation. We want equality—for those principles the National Equal Rights League stands.*

During those early years of black settlement in Johnstown, leaders who came and lived there discussed the race issue frequently. It was at the forefront of much of the black community's collective mind. In 1922, the Reverend G.W. Kincaid addressed the parishioners of Cambria Chapel A.M.E. Zion Church. Kincaid told them that they had to follow a higher example than white people. Kincaid was the most influential black leader in Johnstown. He was outspoken on issues of racism, which was often linked to the theory of social Darwinism.

"As a people, for 250 years, we were enslaved by the white man, and his customs became our customs, good, bad and indifferent, but after 60 years' opportunities to think, I believe it is time for us to select our own grounds of righteousness," Kincaid said, as published in the *Johnstown Tribune*. "If we discover, in our judgment, to follow the white man's precepts and examples is wrong, we should make a different selection. I lay the burden of our guilt upon the white man, as we have aped him for the last 300 years."

The purity of the races was spoken about in Old Johnstown, and they stressed the importance of maintaining it. In March 1921, a speaker came to Johnstown to discuss the matter. A few weeks later, the Reverend Kincaid gave a rebuttal: "The theory of the survival of the fittest is agitating the world more than ever before. But it has changed its significant title to what is known now as 'eugenics,' which means substantially 'well born' or good birth."

Kincaid described in brutal detail how ancient nations used to put to death the weak and decrepit children and permitted only those perceived as

Rosedale children pose for a picture. Children in the neighborhood had a significant number of challenges, including living in close quarters and in segregated schools. *Courtesy of the Johnstown Area Heritage Association.*

the strongest and well-shaped physically to survive. "I do not apply the term 'degeneracy' to the colored people, because degeneracy works back to a type and not away from it in the human family. The average colored American is too near the pure type of his race to be in a very deep degeneracy, but the word must be applied to the mixed races of Aryan (Caucasian) of whom it would be vain to find a pure type except among the Georgians of Asia."

Kincaid said that the argument among many white racists was to preserve the purity of the races by marrying and having the best children possible. He asserted that this was the prevailing view. He also said that black people should watch this and realize it didn't apply to them. "A man who lives in the slums is unfit to live anywhere else, so it is said. A man who is made a million by a turn in the stock market lives in a palace, but he can only write his name to a check. He cannot tell a spade from a rake."

Kincaid added eugenics wasn't the right social rule to follow in determining who should survive: "There is a law of nature here: it is the law of common sense and good government. We are surrounded by conditions best suited for strength and survival, and the conditions which promote weakness, disease and degeneracy are removed or beyond our reach."

Another shot of children in the Rosedale neighborhood. Not many pictures exist to show what life in the community was like. But various newspaper accounts say that it was a hard place to live given the poor housing conditions. *Courtesy of the Johnstown Area Heritage Association.*

He later pointed out that men often don't follow the same rules and laws as the rest of the animals of the world:

> *The great mistake made by many so-called scientific purifiers of the human race is in not being able to separate man with reason from animals or beasts without reasoning powers. There is such a thing as intellectual progress and the betterment of the reasoning faculties, but so long as we limit survivorship to the physical and not the mental powers, we are betraying man into degeneracy instead of helping him out of it.*
>
> *There is one great teacher whose lessons are to be learned and deeply pondered. They lead to an uplift that no money and no medical examination or selection can possibly attain. He was poor and forsaken, rejected by his own, but he was and is the type to be attained. In establishing the highest type possible to man with reasoning powers, he ran counter to the doctrine of the survival of the fittest as men saw it in his day, so they crucified him but too late to efface the type which we must follow or fall into degeneracy.*

Though black people were not seen as equals and had been discriminated against in virtually every aspect of life, they had become part of the fabric in Johnstown, and their journey was much like the other immigrant groups that had come to the city. And much like those other newcomers, there was a resentment toward them that brewed among the people who had been there longer.

BAD ELEMENTS AND BAD REACTIONS

Police records were being smashed during April 1917, Johnstown cops told reporters. They were on pace to arrest more than seven hundred people during that month. Before the Great Migration, arrests averaged around two to four hundred per month. The police said the reason for this increase was the importation of labor from the South and from Mexico.

"Hundreds of men are being brought here every month by the industrial concerns of this city, from every section that has men to furnish," noted the *Johnstown Democrat*. "The laborers imported include many men of questionable habits and inclinations, and the police are kept busy during all hours."

In August 1917, Johnstown chief of police M.W. Swabb proposed to city council members that they purchase more revolvers and ammunition for his police force, which made many within the city's journalistic community think the police were preparing for a possible race riot. Swabb disputed such reports, saying that the guns were only for a reserve supply. As the city's population continued to boom, the force hired and needed to arm more officers.

"The resolution introduced in council asks for only 50 revolvers," Swabb said. "The small number is in itself sufficient proof that the guns are not wanted in anticipation of any race riots or any great disturbances. Fifty revolvers would not go very far in a big riot. The Negroes in this city are not causing any more trouble than the white people. There are bad Negroes, of course, just as there are bad white people. The Negroes are being brought here to help industrial conditions, to solve the labor problem. They are not taking other men's jobs. They are not being brought here as strikebreakers, as they were in St. Louis and in other cities where trouble resulted.

"We are not expecting any trouble from the Negroes. We are not expecting any race riots. The revolvers and ammunition are simply to stock our reserve supply, which has been about exhausted."[12]

Swabb said that newspapers caused alarm within the community. That was needless, he told reporters. He told them that they shouldn't take the law into their own hands. The citizens should trust their police force. He also urged gun merchants not to sell guns to people who did not have a license or a legitimate reason for owning a weapon.

"The idea is to keep cool. The purpose of the police department is to preserve peace and to punish those who violate the law," he said. "Individuals should not try to punish each other. The law will take care of any form of disorder, and the proper place to report any lawlessness is to the police department. Let the law punish the man or woman who violates the law."

But others in the community were a little more wary. Later that year, City Councilman George M. Harshberger presented a resolution asking for $700 to purchase revolvers and ammunition for the police department. Mayor Louis Franke thought it was a good idea.

"There have been upheavals here and there over the country," Franke said, "and we do not know how soon we may be called upon to cope with similar conditions here. We ought to be prepared for an emergency. In case there is need of deputizing a large number of citizens, we would have nothing with which to arm them. All over the country, we hear of unrest among the Negroes coming up from the south. They have organized to protect and aid their people wherever these race riots occur. Our police department is not big enough nor well enough equipped to handle a big riot."[13]

Among the black laborers who moved north were those who drank, fought, killed and assaulted. Many of those types within the black community went to Franklin Borough, which was described in local newspapers as a mecca for the African American criminal element. There they participated in numerous unsavory activities, including playing craps, smoking opium, shooting morphine, snorting cocaine and drinking alcohol.[14] They also drank in the Minersville section of town, which was the evening rendezvous for most Rosedale residents. There weren't any speakeasies in Rosedale itself.[15]

Another dangerous area was known as the Hill, and white men who visited the area were shocked to find black and Mexican men drinking with white women.[16] At the time, interracial relationships shocked white men, and it often led to lynching in the South. The Hill was a red-light district run by organized crime.[17] Criminals from other parts of the country set up their operations there. Murder, robbery, pickpocketing and other scams were not uncommon in that part of Johnstown.

Rosedale itself could be dangerous, especially for women who went there to socialize. Eleanore Smith, a black woman who was a social butterfly, frequented the neighborhood for dances and other parties. She appeared before police court once to discuss what it was like for a young woman.

"If you all is colored and don't live in Rosedale, and you go to a dance in Rosedale and get mixed up with the black trash down there, why you, you is a cut woman—if you is a woman," she was quoted as saying in the *Johnstown Tribune.*

Smith told the court that there were gangs within Rosedale. A gang attacked someone if one of its members were insulted or hurt by someone else. This happened once when Smith went to a party. When she was asked to dance and refused, the man threatened to get his knife and cut her head off. The man was later taken before police court and sentenced.[18]

In those days, Johnstown could be perilous, even for well-respected members of black society. Two men attacked Dr. Moses Clayborne after one of them crashed into his vehicle. Both of the men were drunk and tried to flee. Clayborne jumped on their car to get their names and number. Then they began pummeling him, at which point he beat them both with a wrench.

As Rosedale grew, so too did the need to police it. Mayor Louis Franke, who ran the city from 1916 to 1920, said that neighborhood needed the same level of supervision and protection as any other area.

"We are going to take care of the outlying districts just the same as the heart of town and those who violate the law will find that they will have just as hard a time getting away with it in Rosedale or any other outlying section as they would on Main and Franklin Streets," Franke said to the *Johnstown Tribune* when he decided to increase police presence in the neighborhood amid its explosive population growth.[19]

In February 1918, Chief of Police M.W. Swabb told city council that his department needed more men in uniform and a larger prison to house the people officers arrested: "I cannot refrain from once more urging the need of a larger city prison. This subject is threadbare, but the need is there just the same. The repairs and painting have but camouflaged the real need and by no means changed the increasing demand for it." Of the nearly 3,600 prisoners, most were either black men or European immigrants.

The perception of the new arrivals among Johnstown's longtime population often came from the reported crime statistics. They were seen as troublemakers who cost the taxpayers money to house and feed in Johnstown's jails. That was reflected in speeches given in the community, including one by Oliver P. Bohler, president of the Association of Directors of the Poor and Charities and Correction of Pennsylvania, who was quoted in the *Johnstown Tribune*. "The call of high wages, equality and high living appealed to the honest and dishonest alike, but particularly to the latter, the result being that the vast army of floaters, petty criminals and other undesirable types followed the trend of inducement and landed in the jails and workhouses of the north," Bohler said.

At one point during Franke's tenure, city council discussed the possibility of hiring black police officers to patrol Rosedale. At the time, the department was understaffed, and there was an additional feeling that having black representation in law enforcement might reduce the chance of a race riot.[20] The proposal never became a reality, however, and soon the police force and the black community were at odds.

In December 1918, an officer shot a black man after fearing for his life. The man killed was Joseph Boston, known as the "Bad Man from Texas."

Boston had recently come from the state to Conemaugh Borough. He started trouble early one morning in a boardinghouse in Franklin Borough. Officers arrived on the scene after being called. Chief of Police Daniel Wirick and Officer Patrick Coyle went to the house, each entering by a different door. Coyle was the first to approach Boston, who got angry when the officer tried to arrest him. Boston beat Coyle terribly with his fists. Wirick came to Coyle's rescue, and Boston picked up a chair and struck the chief with it. Boston raved like a maniac throughout the ordeal, according to a newspaper account. Wirick drew his revolver from his pocket and fired four times at Boston, who died.

The officer justified his use of force when he described the man as a giant with superhuman strength. The black man had overpowered two policemen and fought for more than seven minutes before being killed. In the inquest of the shooting, a jury found that the black man had come to his death as a matter of self-defense on the part of the officers.[21]

Headlines reflected white people's suspicion of black citizens. In the February 11, 1919 edition of the *Johnstown Democrat*, a reporter wrote about a black man who wounded his wife in the city. The writer also included commentary about Mexicans in the article. But the headline implied more than the text suggested.

"WAVE OF CRIME SEEMS TO BE SWEEPING CITY; NEGRO IS UNDER ARREST," it read.

White residents also feared a crime wave from the Mexicans. In Johnstown, many newspaper articles linked both black and Mexican workers with the crimes that were committed in the community. The demonization of Mexicans and Mexican Americans is a common occurrence in media, according to Dr. Andrew Sandoval-Strausz.

"It made them subject to violence and abuse. And to eventually be run out of town. It's another fairly consistent condition that white workers will believe falsehoods about people of color," he said. "That's a consistent diet that they're fed of misinformation. Before large-scale acts of violence, whether it be a lynching or running people out of town, the media are accused of whipping people up. That leaves them unable to work and victims to violence. It's awful."

Dr. Spencer Crew said the media tended to focus on the worst aspects of minority communities: "What I found is news about the black community tends to be negative. What you're seeing is newspapers reporting the bad that goes on there, and not so much about the positive things about churches or fraternal organization. It's not necessarily wrong, but it's biased coverage."

Johnstown's newspapers present an interesting case study in how to respond to revolutionary change. While strikers received negative press from Pittsburgh papers, the *Johnstown Democrat* remained neutral. Company officials and unions both criticized the newspapers. Warren Worth Bailey sought to remain objective and print actual news while expressing general opposition to strikes and violence. He wanted to write about the nobler aspects of society. Insofar as black people were concerned, the *Democrat* carried news that was both positive and negative. While journalists wrote about the criminal activities extensively, they also talked about civil rights speeches and movements in the community in a fair, nonhostile and sometimes favorable light. However, the negative coverage was more frequent.

The *Johnstown Tribune* was more conservative. It opposed anarchism, Bolshevism and unionism. It supported the steel companies. Strikers described the paper and its journalists as tools of industry. When the *Tribune* wrote about African Americans, the stories generally had to do with the lurid details of their lives, including crimes, love triangles and other shocking aspects of the community.

In 1920, a sixty-eight-year-old woman was murdered in her home near Hinckston Dam. Her grandson found her dead, stabbed in the abdomen and

The Johnstown Tribune Building, located at 425 Locust Street, housed the Republican newspaper in the city that was run by Anderson Walters, a one-time congressman. *Library of Congress, Prints and Photographs Division, Washington, D.C.*

in one eye. Neighbors told police that schoolchildren as well as the woman had seen a black person about the place several times.

That same year, W.E. Cephas, a leader in the black community, accused Johnstown police officer W.J. Kirby of felonious assault. Kirby was standing on the Minersville Bridge when two women came to him and told him black men had insulted them. He went to the Cephas home to look for them, but he was met with resistance, according to his court testimony. Cephas went to the telephone to call the chief of police. Kirby, thinking Cephas was going for a gun, pulled his revolver out. Kirby later became unruly and pushed a man downstairs, according to the accusation. Kirby was acquitted of the charges.

Later in 1920, Marshall Tillman, a thirty-year-old black man, murdered his wife with a heavy axe at their home in Prospect, a neighborhood in Johnstown. She died at Memorial Hospital less than three hours after he chopped her over the head. Walking quietly into the police station, Tillman, a large man clad in a suit of overalls, calmly laid a razor, knife and Cambria Steel Company workman's check on the desk of the warden and said, "I just done killed my wife, lock me up."[22] Tillman had been an off-and-on-again employee for Cambria Steel for some time and had lived in Johnstown for a while.

The bold headline of the story that ran in the *Johnstown Tribune* singled out his race:

Negro Slays Wife with Axe
Chops open back of her head as she attempts to escape from Him

Such headlines were common when the article dealt with black criminals. When members of the white community perpetrated similar crimes, their race was largely left out of the reporting. The impression left on many of Johnstown's white population was that race had something to do with it.

"Newspapers built up the crime wave of black migrants," Dr. Charles Lumpkins said. "They wanted to rape white women. They wanted to buy guns. I have no other way to corroborate those headlines to statistics. I have to take it not with a grain of salt, but with some skepticism. I don't know about Johnstown, but I have a feeling that racism was an underlying issue."

Lumpkins added that there was an element of white supremacy to instances in which race was included in crime reports.

"I've seen that with other cities. There's a political dimension with it," Lumpkins said. "There are some real criminal justice issues. But newspapers were being highly selective, when they had this preponderant focus on black people. Something else was going on. Something political."

During the early years of the Great Migration, there were reports of black men accosting white women, which struck a raw nerve with many white men in Johnstown. In reporting on a crime in October 1921 involving the brutal rape and murder of a young girl, the *Johnstown Democrat* needlessly speculated on what segment of the population the perpetrator came from by mentioning a popular hangout for black people.

"That corner is on the direct route to Rosedale and daily many Negroes, who came here from the south in the latter days of the war, pass back and forth," the *Democrat* wrote. "From time to time a good many Negroes gather in the barroom of the hotel at the corner. The police have no evidence to attach the frightful crime to any of these Negroes, but no effort will be spared to find the fiend who could have conceived and carried out so shocking a crime."

The police search, unsurprisingly, focused on the black community after that.

Racial hatred in the country had grown during that time. Nationally, the Ku Klux Klan experienced a rebirth. It was inspired in part by the release of *The Birth of a Nation*, a 1915 film that adapted a Thomas Dixon novel called *The Clansman*. The film depicts freed slaves destroying property and attempting to rape white women, all with the support and conspiracy of Northern carpetbaggers. In the movie, the Klan is portrayed as the protector of white womanhood. Another publication that led to the organization's revival was *The Protocols of the Elders of Zion*; its printing in the United States was funded by Henry Ford. The document is a forgery that claims to recount a nineteenth-century meeting where Jewish people discussed how to control the world through finances and the media. Both inspired Klansmen. William Joseph Simmons, a southerner who fought in the Spanish-American War, saw the movie. Simmons was a drifter who worked odd jobs as a salesman, teacher and paid organizer. While the film moved him, he was also fascinated with the lynching of Leo Frank, a Jewish man from Atlanta who was wrongfully blamed for the murder of a young white girl.

He got a copy of the Ku Klux Klan's original *Prescript* and used it along with Masonic rites to create a new ritual that emphasized the hatred and fear of African Americans. But it also directed anger toward communism, socialism and immigrants. Simmons wasn't much of an organizer. He collected only a few hundred Klansmen in the first five years. It wasn't until he met some experienced public relations professionals that his luck changed. Elizabeth Tyler and Edward Young Clarke, owners of the Southern Publicity Association, helped to promote the Klan. Clarke's father had been a colonel in the Confederate army and owned the *Atlanta Constitution*. They saw a potentially lucrative client.

"The minute we said Ku Klux Klan," Tyler said at one point, "editors from all over the United States began literally pressing us for publicity."

Clarke and Tyler convinced Simmons that his organization could reach a national audience. Simmons signed a contract with the publicists that gave them 80 percent of all the money from new recruits into the Klan. In effect, they were head of the Klan for two years. They turned Simmons into a good speaker who emphasized that degenerative forces were destroying America. The Klansmen expanded the targets of their wrath to include Jewish people, Catholics, immigrants and big-city people who were enthralled with the Jazz Age. The Klan hated people from parts of Europe that weren't Anglo-Saxon,

Colonel William Joseph Simmons, imperial wizard of the Ku Klux Klan, seated at a table during House committee investigation of the organization in 1921. Simmons was not a very successful Klan leader until he received help from the Southern Publicity Association. After one of the most successful marketing efforts in history, his name and likeness were known throughout the country. *Library of Congress, Prints and Photographs Division, Washington, D.C.*

namely Greeks and Italians. Simmons was a good interview subject, and he was effective at spinning the Klan's side of things, according to author Linda Gordon's history of the early years of the organization's rebirth in her book *The Second Coming of the KKK: The Ku Klux Klan of the 1920s*. Clarke and Tyler placed advertisements in newspapers and presented memberships to ministers for free. By January 1921, they had deployed over 1,000 new recruiters across the country and grew the Klan by 850,000 new members.

Johnstown's black leaders responded to the national white supremacist movement. Under the leadership of Dr. G.W. Kincaid, the Cambria Chapel A.M.E. Zion Church in Johnstown adopted a resolution condemning the Klan in the early 1920s. "We, your committee, wish to commend the National Government, including Congress, for the active part they are taking in putting an end to the Ku Klux Klan, whose head is Joseph Simmons, of Atlanta, Georgia, the 'Imperial Wizard,'" the resolution read.

It continued, "Be it resolved, that we, your committee, call upon each minister and delegate here assembled to write to their Senator and Congressman for their full support in this investigation now going on to establish the right of this Klan, who is going around terrorizing, shooting down high officials and taking charge independent of the courts of our country."

On September 22, 1921, a resolution was passed at the Cambria Chapel A.M.E. Zion Church urging Johnstown's congressmen "to use their influence in any way to vote for a measure for a thorough investigation of the infamous Klan."

In the November 1922 edition of the *Dawn*, a publication of the Ku Klux Klan, Clarke wrote about the organization's beliefs regarding where white and black citizens stood in the grand scheme of America.

"There is not one particle of scientific evidence to prove 'that all men are created equal.' It is a vicious dogma. It stifles racial pride and deadens the most vital urges known to mankind—self-preservation and self-expansion," Clarke said. "The false doctrine, championed by certain racial elements in this country in which Anglo-Saxons have little in common, is like an insidious disease, slowly consuming the racial individuality of a people to whom this Republic rightly belongs."

The Klan decried the idea of a melting pot. Its membership resisted any attempts to introduce new religions or ethnicities to the country. Klansmen advocated selective immigration. Unlimited immigration sickened them. Though black people were their most frequent target, they vilified Mexicans for being irreligious and criminal.

The KKK in Johnstown, pictured in the 1920s on Bedford Street, organized faster there than anywhere else in the state, according to newspaper accounts at the time. Ostentatious cross burnings and church invasions were part of their recruitment efforts in the city and elsewhere in the commonwealth. *Courtesy of the Johnstown Area Heritage Association.*

One of the drawbacks of living in Johnstown for black and Mexican residents was the large number of Ku Klux Klan members there. In the 1920s, Pennsylvania saw persistent growth of the Klan. And its members were violent. Most Klan organizers made little effort to keep the illiterate and hoodlum elements out. Though newspapers criticized the Klan, the publicity only served to bolster membership.

Dr. Crew said that the Klan's presence inhibited African Americans from voting and changing the status quo. In states like Pennsylvania near the Mason-Dixon line, the rebirth of the Klan was particularly strong.

"These are states closest to the South," Dr. Crew added. "Southern Pennsylvania, Southern Indiana. That's where they have the greatest revival. Anything they can do to discourage the influx of new people into the communities, that's what they're trying to accomplish."

The Klan arrived in the state early in 1921 with F.W. Atkins in charge. The organization established offices in Philadelphia with a staff of five. Progress was slow. The leadership decided expansion might go faster if they recruited in several points in the state. Two men, Sam D. Rich and a Mr. Faulkner, as his assistant, were sent to the western province headquartered in Pittsburgh. They rented an office in the Jenkins Arcade building. The sign read "Advertising and Publicity" on the door.[23]

The movement was unsuccessful for the first five months in both divisions of the state. They could hardly pay the rent. Their outsider status didn't help with recruitment. The best plan was to sit in their offices and use field organizers, including A.L. Cotton. Able to tell a story with a flourish and built like a football tackle, Cotton had everything Rich was looking for. He went to Erie, north of Pittsburgh, to apprentice. But he was met with stiff opposition following locals' reactions to his recruitment methods, which he wouldn't divulge to reporters or other people. Police arrested Cotton, and he served a short sentence, which made him a martyr.

Cotton soon became successful. He directed the organization in several counties and had a staff of workers. The western province of Pennsylvania had a faster recruitment than the eastern part. Klan leaders in each community highlighted the specific ideas of the national party that appealed the most to locals, according to John Craig's *The Ku Klux Klan in Western Pennsylvania, 1921–1928*. An especially strong unit was organized in Johnstown.

To assist recruiters, the state and national offices of the Klan attained several speakers who pledged themselves to fill engagements. Many were ministers who found the payment a welcome addition to their salaries. Those men were generally the most successful. They emphasized fervent anthems to glorify the Constitution and pure Americanism. They described white Protestants as the underdog and oppressed sufferer.

During the years following the war, there was an economic downturn in southwestern Pennsylvania. The natives and soldiers wanted the same jobs given to immigrants and southern migrants. The Klan realized that it could inflame the hatreds of those groups losing their positions.

The Klan targeted Presbyterian ministers for membership. The Klan leaders felt they would have an easier time recruiting members in churches if the higher-ups got in with that group. The ministers' presence aroused less controversy and opposition from other recruiters and from the public in general. They didn't have to hide their support for the organization. The Klan sent letters to local officials saying they had organized to combat bootleggers and Prohibition violators. Some in the towns in the region thought the organization would help clear some of the vice.

The Klan's appeal was in its dedication to militaristic discipline and white masculinity. The recruiters and publicists for the Klan portrayed members as the epitome of true American manhood. They were knightly, according to their marketing materials. After the Klan had conducted its first activities

Right: Klansmen Sam D. Rich and L.A. Mueller in August 1925. Rich was an important leader in Pennsylvania's Klan. *Library of Congress, Prints and Photographs Division, Washington, D.C.*

Below: The Ku Klux Klan marches down the street in Wilkinsburg, a neighborhood in Pittsburgh, in the 1920s. The Klan grew rapidly in states near the Mason-Dixon line. Both men and women in the area joined branches that grew based on their focus on local intolerances and issues. *Courtesy of the Detre Library & Archives, Senator John Heinz History Center.*

in communities in dramatic, mysterious and spectacular fashion, it created excitement and curiosity among the people living there. Recruitment came much easier afterward. Cross burnings were the most popular form of activity, but church invasions were another common tactic. The Klan ostentatiously gave a cleric an amount of money that was to be used for the religious order's missions. The Klan presented itself as an upholder of the law. It wasn't against police or the courts. It supported them. The Klan wanted people to believe anything it did was legal.

The Johnstown Klan presented itself as a charitable endeavor. In one ceremony at the YWCA on Somerset Street, a number of cars pulled up in front of the building. In single file, the Klansmen came in, presented an envelope with $75, which would be around $950 in today's value, and a pamphlet describing their purpose. The gift had been promised by the YWCA officials for the whole week as the big feature for the opening of its autumn rally. The Klansmen left without receiving the thanks prepared by a woman who worked there.

At Beulah United Evangelical Church in Dale Borough earlier in 1923, fifteen hooded Klansmen entered the church in the middle of the service and gave the Reverend P.L. Griffiths fifty dollars for the church's building fund.

Rumors spread over the years that the headquarters of the Klan in that part of the state, just outside Pittsburgh, was in Johnstown. That branch apparently seemed to be where nearby Altoona and Indiana's units stemmed from. Some estimated the number of Klan members in Johnstown to be 1,500 strong. Johnstown had "Klan Days" in the 1920s, which occasionally brought 30,000 Klansmen and their families to Luna Park. Johnstown was among the first in the state to establish Klavaliers, the military branch of the Klan. The operating methods of the Klan were simple.

"Are you 100 percent American?" the prospective member was asked.

If he said yes, the interrogator would hand out a little card.

"Just look that over," he remarked. "You probably are interested."[24]

If the prospect desired to join the order, he filled out the card with his personal history and returned it to the person from whom it was received. If three Klan members approved it, he was admitted. The initiation fee was said to be six dollars.

Both of Johnstown's newspapers condemned Klan activity. The *Tribune* described the organization as designing. "Whatever is done in the name of such institutions, which contravenes law and order, is usually done by irresponsible persons, acting under malicious leadership," read one editorial.

The *Johnstown Tribune* possessed a great deal of information regarding the intimate and private details of the proceedings, differences and other aspects of the local Klan. Whether some newspaper reporters were members or whether the information was leaked to them is unknown. But they knew what was going on in the local Klavern and reported it to the public. The *Tribune*'s editors said they gathered the information in honest ways.

"If men or women choose to accept membership in these organizations, they should narrowly watch those placed in leadership," the paper said. "They should keep close tab on men, or women, who seek to profit, either in politics or business, from leadership or influence over weak or corrupt leaders. That influence may come from outside the organization."

The Klan had a penchant for burning crosses near Johnstown. In August 1922, Cambria County saw a public demonstration—three loud explosions at three intervals as light blazed up a fiery cross on Green Hill. It was located just above the Johnstown Brick & Tile Company. The cross was a short distance away from the big electric sign of Galliker's Ice Cream Company.

It was the first cross ever burned in the county. With the first view of the cross, after the explosions attracted the attention of many, thousands swarmed the downtown section of the city and gazed at the Klansmen surrounding it. They had their arms extended in exultation as the embers burned the cloth on the cross. The black-clad figure in front was the master of ceremonies, the head of the Klan in the Cambria County District.

A few people attempted to get close to the burning symbol, but police, who had blocked some of the roads to the hill, told them that they could not get on the grounds during the ceremonies. Following the occasion, the

The first cross burning in Johnstown, in August 1922, attracted hundreds of viewers, who watched a weird and cult-like scene on a hill near town. The Ku Klux Klan allegedly had some of the community's most prominent and influential men as its members. Photo first appeared in the *Johnstown Tribune.*

Klansmen entered automobiles and left quickly in darkness. The morning after, hundreds of people made their way to the scene, where the Klansmen had left the cross along with several bags of cotton. Nothing much else of interest was found. One of the Klan members told the newspaper that they were nonpolitical and growing in Cambria County.

Some of Johnstown's most prominent men were part of the local Klan chapter, according to rumors heard by newspaper reporters within the community. They had been initiated at a ceremony under the light of a fiery cross. But who they were remained a secret, as everything and everyone in the Klan was shrouded in secrecy. One later newspaper report indicated that Mayor Cauffiel was a Klansman in the local Klavern during his second administration, which began in 1920. The local newspapers never published the names of any KKK organizers, officers, members or affiliated organizations. The Klan controlled several thousand votes in Johnstown and sent out pamphlets on whom they recommended for public office in the Republican primaries.

Many within Johnstown were not trained to cull the demagoguery from rhetoric or even to suspect it. The average white Johnstown dweller swallowed such pronouncements whole. Gullible people thought the spokespeople were as credible as a professor.

And the news reports of crime fueled racial tension further in 1923. In the summer, a rash of crime dominated Rosedale. Almost always, it was black-on-black crime. Two Rosedale black women got into a fight, and one chased the other with a razor. Fighting and shooting were also crimes in which charges were filed. In mid-August, John Knox was shot and killed in a Rosedale barbershop. It was said that six other black men, who were either charged with accessory to the fact or being suspicious, hid Frank Williams, the alleged murderer.

In June, a black man attacked a fifteen-year-old girl named Catherine Wazniack on the wooded section of the road between Conemaugh and Headrick's Cemetery. He came from behind her and dragged her from the road. She had managed to get away but suffered serious emotional strain. The incident prompted the Ku Klux Klan to go into East Conemaugh and burn a cross as a warning.

By that time, African American residents of Johnstown were fed up with the hostility, prejudice and discrimination. In February 1923, some black people residing in Conemaugh objected to the posting of a sign reading "For Whites Only" at the New York Lunch Room. Some black residents bombarded the hot dog shop with bricks. Fearing a race riot might follow, police were called to the scene. They found no trace of civil unrest. An hour after that trouble, there was a little excitement at the restaurant of W.B. Goughnour, also of Conemaugh. Two black men visited the restaurant and ordered sandwiches they refused to pay for. The waitress said they wouldn't get food until they did. An argument followed. A white man who was in the restaurant told them they had not paid the woman. The black men called him a liar, and they got in an altercation. The feeling was tense in the community for the rest of that day.

Robert Young was among the bad characters within the black community. Born in Carlisle, Kentucky, in 1891, he came to Johnstown as an employee of the Cambria Steel Works. Before coming to the city, he had been employed in Youngstown, Ohio. Rumors persisted throughout the parts of Johnstown that knew him that he had a criminal record in Alabama, where he lived after moving from Kentucky. Some said he had been a killer down there but had been released on parole. He lived in Rosedale since May 1923. Prior to that, he was in the hollow above the community.

The remnants of the once mighty Rosedale Coke Works behind Cambria City in Johnstown. *Photo by the author.*

Today, if you stand along the Honan Avenue Trail, you can see the rolling hills and area that Young lived in. There's a gap between nearby peaks that shows the towering Gothic churches of Cambria City. A scenic waterfall that dumps water into a creek running between Benshoff Road and Honan Avenue captivates hikers who pass by. The only indication that industry and a community existed there are the decrepit pillars that once upheld the coke plant. The catacombs in which people labored are now covered by overgrown brush and knotweed.

Young caused considerable trouble and had domestic difficulties. His wife, Rose, flirted and messed around with other men in Rosedale and Franklin Borough. Repeatedly watching it put him on edge and drove him to drink. It was just a matter of time before disaster struck.

THE SPARK

Robert Young seethed with anger at the idea of his wife sleeping with another man. He thought about it ever since he saw her with other men. They got into an argument at around 8:00 p.m. on the night of Thursday, August 30, 1923. The next-door neighbor, H.R. Samuels, called the police about the yelling.

Sensing trouble, Young left Rosedale in an ugly temper with his buddy Levi Samuels to drink liquor, do drugs and play cards in Franklin Borough, according to an investigation later conducted by the state. Officer Joseph Grachan went to Young's house on Rosedale Street after hearing the report of a disturbance. Rose told Grachan that everything was fine, so he went back on patrol. Word reached Young later that an officer had looked for him.

Young and Samuels returned after consuming a healthy amount of moonshine.[25] The two argued. Young yelled at him to stop and asked that he take him back to Franklin Borough. En route, their car ran into a telegraph pole in Rosedale. Young was thrown against the glass, which cut his face. Grachan went to the car to investigate.

"You're the bastard that was going to arrest me," Young said before pulling out a gun and shooting Grachan in the chest, tearing a hole at least three inches in diameter in his police coat and slightly burning two letters in his inside pocket.[26] A struggle ensued. The policeman pulled his revolver from its holster and emptied the cylinder. Knowing that he was wounded, the officer broke loose and went to a nearby restaurant, where he called for aid. A man named Meyers telephoned police headquarters.

Samuels ran and told his father what had happened. His dad called the police, and a detail of officers and detectives went to Rosedale. Among them was Captain Otto Fink, Lieutenant William Bender and Officer John Yoder. Fink was in command.

Young, in the meantime, started for H.R. Samuels's house. The doors had been barred, but Young broke open the front entrance and went through the residence hunting for his wife. Samuels informed him that she was not there, but Young kept yelling for her while looking under beds in every room. He left a few minutes later and went to his own home. Another woman who stayed there heard him coming and locked the door to her room. Young went to the top of the second floor and fired a number of shots through the door. The woman screamed. The police who just responded heard the bullets.

It was shortly before eleven o'clock at night that County Detective John A. James called up the *Johnstown Democrat*. James was known as

County Detective John A. James.   Special Officer Joseph Abrahams.

Two of the officers who were involved in the shooting. The crime outraged the Johnstown community, and it led to talk of destroying Rosedale, the black neighborhood in town. The shooting was the culmination of years of racial tension following the Great Migration. Photos first appeared in the *Johnstown Tribune*.

one of the most fearless officers in Cambria County. Always a friend of the newspapers, he helped reporters piece together many stories when information would have been practically impossible to get through other sources. James told a journalist that he had received a report about a shooting in Rosedale.

"You will hear from me in a short time," the detective said. James and Joseph Abrahams, an assistant city assessor, drove another car to the scene.

Young hid between two shanties following his encounter with Grachan. Fink traveled to the extreme end of Rosedale, just opposite the last house, to turn the car around. As they drove the police car under an arc light near a boardinghouse, Young opened fire. Fink was shot in the back, partially paralyzed as a result, and Bender was shot in the abdomen. Officer Otto Nukem, picked up on the way to Rosedale, was hit in the left arm.

They thought there were two gunmen. With Fink and Bender down, Nukem kept the car between him and the stream of shots. He climbed the embankment at the side of the road, out of range.

"It was so dark that we couldn't make out the forms of the gunmen, although I'm sure there were two Negroes," he later told a reporter. "We didn't have a chance. The firing started the very instant we got out of the car, and I guess that I was lucky to stop only one of the bullets in the rain of shots—I don't know how many—that were fired before we realized what we were up against."

James and Abrahams arrived on the scene. They found Grachan in a nearby restaurant. Employees were roughly dressing his wound. When they had the clumsy bandages tied into place as best they could, Grachan, pale and weak from loss of blood, struggled to get up.

"Let me have my gun back and I'll go out and get 'em," he told James and Abrahams.

With instructions to the restaurant owner to keep Grachan inside the building until the ambulance arrived, James and Abrahams went to the place where they thought Young sought shelter. Yoder joined them. They found the door closed. Pressing against it, James and Abrahams forced it open.

As they broke into the room, Young opened with another volley of shots and shot James and Abrahams. James fell against Yoder. Abrahams staggered to the street before he fell, seriously wounded.

Young left through the back door, but he met Yoder around the side of the home. Both fired weapons. They went up and down the avenue, around the shanties and through a house. It lasted for a while.

Capt. of Police Otto Fink.   Patrolman Joseph Grachan.

When the officers were taken to the hospital, the residents of Johnstown and reporters covering it closely monitored every development regarding their health. The *Johnstown Tribune* began a fundraising drive to help the cops who were involved in the shootout with Robert Young. Photos first appeared in the *Johnstown Tribune*.

Yoder ran out of ammunition, went to the wounded officers to retrieve another gun and again took up the chase. Young ran out of ammunition and took a gun from one of the wounded officers. Within a few yards of where James and Abrahams were wounded, Yoder shot Young through the chest. Young staggered a few feet and fell dead near Lieutenant Bender.

Young's body remained there until early the next morning. Police were preoccupied with keeping order.

Ambulances rushed to Rosedale shortly before midnight to take the injured officers to Memorial Hospital, except Grachan, whom paramedics took to Mercy Hospital. Detective James and Officer Abrahams died just as they reached Memorial.

When the surviving officers got there, every bed was taken. Several patients less seriously ill relinquished their rooms, and the officers were placed in private quarters. No stone was left unturned in the effort to save their lives.[27]

Lieut. William H. Bender.

Detective Otto Nukem.

Above: The black community disavowed its connection to the officer shootings. Robert Young didn't reflect their values or belief in treating the authorities with respect. Photos first appeared in the *Johnstown Tribune*.

Right: John Yoder was the man who fatally shot Robert Young. While other officers hadn't fared as well, Yoder was able to avoid being killed. Photos first appeared in the *Johnstown Tribune*.

Detective John Yoder.

Following the crime, there were reports of a second shooter. Officers focused on capturing or shooting him.

Police later arrested four black men and two black women who were walking in a group on Hinckston Avenue in Rosedale. After policemen approached the six, the suspects said they had done no wrong. Police searched them and found no weapons. Still, they took them in.

Johnstown police headquarters was at fever heat. Officers came in from throughout the city and went to Rosedale in taxicabs. They took riot guns from the police station. First reports said that more than a dozen black men took part in a gun battle and that they had ambushed half a dozen police officers, killing several. Police rounded up fifteen black suspects, including two women, and held them pending an investigation.

Crowds surged before the jail holding the suspects. It forced the police to take the arrested black men and women to a secret place of confinement. Later, the arrested men and women were discharged without any charges.

Bender told reporters about the events while at the hospital. "We could see nothing, except the spitting of revolvers from the dark," he said. "We were at police headquarters when the telephone call came from Rosedale for the patrol and ambulances. Who had been injured we didn't stop to learn. The patrol went ahead, and Capt. Fink, Detectives John Yoder, William Courtney and myself followed in the city's Buick. We heard the reports of revolvers as we neared the colony and went immediately to the scene of the shooting—at the extreme end of Hinckston Avenue."

Bender said the situation was like a riot.

"The Negroes, and there must have been many of them shooting from the bunkhouse and from behind it, could see us as our car passed under a light on the street," Bender said. They were evidently waiting for us. As soon as our car came to a stop, Fink jumped out and went into the house. There was shooting on every side of us. Fink had gone only a minute or so when the cry went up that he had been shot.

"At the same time they opened fire on us. The whole thing was happening so quickly that, with Fink shot and bullets showering on us, we had barely gotten away from the car. We couldn't see. The firing came from utter blackness. We saw that, and then I was shot."

He spoke about a brush with Young.

"They didn't lay me low," Bender said. "After the shooting at us, a Negro emerged within 12 feet of us. We could barely see him. I had been wounded, but still stood on my feet, and leveling my gun at the Negro, I shot. I feel certain I hit him at least once. He was so close to me that I could hardly have missed him. He still stood, however, and John Yoder finished him. We were all shooting at whatever Negroes we could see in action."

Detective Otto Nukem also didn't believe it was one man.

"The patrol went ahead and Fink, Bender and the others followed in a Buick," Nukem said. "They left me in charge at headquarters, with orders to send as many men as possible to Rosedale. We were expecting Jack James and Abrahams in the office any minute. I waited for them and when they arrived, the three of us went immediately to Rosedale. Joe was driving and he backed his car the length of the street to the bunkhouse where most of the trouble was.

"No one who wasn't there will ever realize what an awful ambush we were caught in. We couldn't see a thing and bullets flew about us from all directions. We didn't know where we were or what was going on. And everything happened in an instant—before we could get our bearings."

Both Bender and Nukem told reporters of black people emerging from the darkness of bushes in the rear of the bunkhouse, emptying their revolvers and returning to the pitch-blackness to reload. They both thought the assailants had a store of ammunition to the rear of the bunkhouse. Though the real story was that it was a lone gunman, people believed that multiple shooters had been involved once Bender's and Nukem's accounts appeared in the *Johnstown Tribune* the next day.

FEVER HEAT

Several hundred white residents of nearby neighborhoods crowded into the streets of Rosedale, and police dispersed them with difficulty. They feared further trouble between whites and blacks. When news reached Johnstown that two officers had been killed and three or four severely wounded, people presumed there was a race riot. The white citizens congregated around city hall and said that they would "burn up the town" to gain some sense of justice.

People talked like that about Rosedale and other black settlements. Some people planned on "cleaning out every damned Negro settlement in town," according to one newspaper reporter.

Talk of a mob, or the Ku Klux Klan, raiding the Rosedale settlement on the night following the shooting brought action from police headquarters. Preparing for an uprising against the black residents, the state police, augmented by more than fifty officers and plainclothesmen, were placed on duty in Rosedale to patrol the district. The night passed quietly.[28]

A reporter for the *Meyersdale Republic*, which was based in a town near Johnstown, wrote about the shooting and said he hoped other towns wouldn't experience the dangers of moonshine liquor and reckless men like Robert Young. "Nothing but deep sympathy is felt for the families of the men who were killed, and for the men themselves, as well as their families, who were wounded," the reporter commented. "All the men who were shot were heads of families and highly regarded, substantial citizens. Such men often must bear the brunt of criminal tendencies inflamed by liquor, especially poisonous moonshine liquor."

On August 31, vast throngs of people congregated near the post office. Hundreds eagerly sought to see the bullet marks on the patrol wagon.

In the absence of Police Chief Charles E. Briney, who had been in Pittsburgh attending the police chiefs' convention, Councilman Thomas J. Harris and City Detective George Patterson took charge of the police.

Later, at 5:30 p.m., the body of Joseph Abrahams was laid to rest in the Jewish plot in Geistown. Hundreds of friends attended the ceremonial services that took place at his home. Abrahams had been connected with the police department since 1906 and figured in many important cases. He was fluent in multiple languages, which made him a valuable witness in many criminal trials. He left behind a widow and four children.

Robert Young's body was at the undertaking establishment of George Viering and was later interned at Sandyvale Cemetery. A bullet shattered his left arm above the elbow, his breast was pierced above the heart and a bullet had gone through his left thigh. No one attended his funeral. The undertaker wired his father, Benjamin Young, for instructions about the body.[29]

During that evening, people lined the sidewalks between Main and Locust Streets near the market. They eagerly watched all movements at police headquarters. Several officers were stationed at the alley adjacent to city hall to keep the crowds back.

Although the trend of the conversations heard among the assemblage was menacing, the crowds were peaceable and there was little trouble. Every available officer was stationed at an entrance to the area where the shooting happened. And avenues to Rosedale were guarded. Police closely questioned all pedestrians about their business in that section of the city.

The county sheriff and a number of his deputies visited Rosedale. Six state troopers from Greensburg, a town an hour to the west, arrived and were on duty during the night. More troopers came later.

The county's presiding judge postponed any criminal cases for September court because District Attorney D.P. Weimer asked for a delay following the deaths of James and Abrahams, who possessed evidence in the trials. Police officials and attorneys from the district attorney's office prepared a number of criminal cases in which James and Abrahams were to testify. James's successor would not be appointed at once, Weimer told newspaper reporters. County Detective Ed Whited of Barnesboro handled the situation until a replacement came.[30]

On Saturday, two policemen still fought for their lives at Memorial and Mercy Hospitals, with little chance for recovery. A statement was issued that there was no change in the condition of Fink, who was shot through the spine. He couldn't move his legs. And it was feared he would not live for more than a few hours.[31]

Dr. J.B. Lowman treated Fink and was helping the captain stage a desperate fight for his life. Dr. J.W. Jefferson attended to Lieutenant Bender while Dr. J.B. McAneny looked after Grachan.

Grachan was in Mercy Hospital with a bullet wound in his right lung, and physicians entertained little hope for recovery. Doctors operated on him to remove the bullet, but Grachan was so weak that doctors abandoned the effort.

Fink and Bender were quartered in one of the most attractive rooms in Memorial Hospital, where they had the benefit of plenty of light and air. Two special nurses gave every aid to the injured officers. Because of the seriousness of Fink's condition, he had no visitors.

Bender had showed an excellent chance of surviving from his bullet wound in the abdomen. Nukem, shot in the left arm, was discharged from the hospital.

Memorial Hospital superintendent William J. Finn said the public was coming to understand the sacrifice on the part of police officers—their eagerness to dash headlong into danger and their disregard for their own lives in the discharge of their perilous duty.

"The entire personnel at Memorial Hospital feels keenly the misfortune which has befallen the community and through sympathy and consideration are proving the intense admiration of the citizens for those who uphold its laws," Finn told the *Tribune*.[32]

The newspapers carried front-page fundraising efforts that helped pay the officers' medical bills. Warren Worth Bailey of the *Johnstown Democrat* donated twenty-five dollars. He asked Johnstown residents to contribute regardless of how small the sum. The *Democrat* gave the money to a committee appointed by the mayor and the chief of police.

"Two officers died that all might live in peace and safety in Johnstown," the *Democrat* said in the article announcing the fundraiser. "Johnstown owes a debt to their families that money alone can never repay."

The newspaper's editorial board also penned an op-ed about the tragedy, saying news of the officers' deaths stunned the whole city. They said the shooting was unprecedented and the guilt resided solely with the lone gunman. The newspaper then praised each one of the individual officers.

"People's sympathy likewise goes out to the families of the dead officers as well as to those of the wounded," it read. "There is not a home in Johnstown which is indifferent to their bereavement, their sorrow and their anxiety."

After police questioned a few suspects, they determined that Young acted alone. Chief of Police Charles Briney told the *Johnstown Tribune* that nearly thirty black people had been taken into custody by that time, and detectives had grilled them before being released.

"No one is being held in connection with the shooting in Rosedale," Briney said. "We arrested and brought to City Hall for questioning a score of men and women. Our investigation convinces us that none of them had anything to do with the affair, and confirmed our first theory that only one man, Robert Young, who was killed, was involved."

Shortly after the officers finished the investigation, black residents of Rosedale sent W.E. Cephas to the *Johnstown Democrat's* office with a letter.

"The respectable and law abiding colored residents of Rosedale wish to publicly express their profound regret for the recent deplorable outbreaks of lawlessness which have deeply disgraced this section of the city," the statement read. "We wish especially to express sincere condolences to the families, relatives and friends of the brave officers who were murdered and to those who were injured at their post of duty."

They feared guilt by association.

"We want it publicly known that the respectable colored people here take no part whatever with murderers and other criminals of our race. We rightly regard them as a disgrace to us and as a danger to any community," the letter continued. "We trust that these assassins will be speedily brought to justice and given their just sentence and the maximum penalty the law allows."

As the officers fought for their lives and tumult surrounded city hall, the Ku Klux Klan burned a cross above Rosedale on Minersville Hill as a warning to the black residents. People in Minersville as well as Cambria City and parts of Westmont were attracted to the symbol, which was ablaze around 10:00 p.m. the night after the shooting. The cross was plainly visible from the central part of the city and burned for nearly ten minutes.

THE OVERLORD

Watching all of this was Mayor Joseph E. Cauffiel. Cauffiel, over six feet tall, stout and combative in every look and action, was central to Johnstown civic life. Cauffiel also was a stormy figure in Cambria County politics. He was known as a ruddy, thundering desk-pounder and given the nickname of "Fighting Joe."

Anti-corruption and anti-vice crusades were the hallmark of his first foray into the political realm. Prior to his start in politics, Cauffiel criticized various councilmen in Johnstown for reported conflicts of interest in awarding contracts to utility companies the council members had a vested interest in. In his first campaign in 1911, Cauffiel promised to rid the police force of grafters and political operatives. He offered the chief of police position to a preacher who had argued for more morality within local law enforcement. Cauffiel became mayor in 1912.

The citizens of Johnstown reelected Cauffiel in 1920 after one intervening term by Mayor Louis Franke. A strike had been in progress in the steelworks, and Cauffiel's reelection campaign was aided by the discontent caused by it along with the support of so-called patriotic societies.

After reelection, he told the local Kiwanis Club that he wanted to make English the official language of Johnstown, and he hoped to make it spoken through force of law. Cauffiel garnered support by vilifying foreigners, Mexicans and black people. In his inaugural address, he took it a step further.

"No meetings should be permitted within the city limits where any language other than the English is spoken," he told those who came to hear him.

Peoples' Candidate
FOR GOVERNOR

JOS. CAUFFIEL
MAYOR OF JOHNSTOWN

Only Republican Candidate Opposed
to Penrose, Booze and Gang Rule
Vote for Cauffiel and Restore Peoples' Rights

Joseph Cauffiel campaigned as a reformer who would rid the city of vice and corruption. He took on the public utility companies and liquor peddlers. *Courtesy of the Johnstown Area Heritage Association.*

"Adoption of the English language will be the first step toward Americanizing foreign-born citizens. We can then educate them to the principles of the city, state and nation.

"As officials of the city, we should insist upon all foreign-born becoming naturalized as soon as the statute laws will permit. By doing this, those of alien birth will take greater pride in the interests of the city and will be better citizens in every way."

He was a reformer in Johnstown politics and a friend of Teddy Roosevelt, having received a delegate position during the memorable Bull Moose Convention in 1912. Pennsylvania governor Gifford Pinchot counted Cauffiel as a friend. When he was sworn in to his second four-year term in 1920 as Johnstown's mayor, he set his sights on the booze taking over the region.

Cauffiel was married to Rebecca Brinton Sellers, a teacher in the Franklin Borough Schools. They had four daughters and a son. Those who loved him praised him for his vision and quick mind. His daughter Eleanor Cauffiel Rutledge later wrote a tribute to him.

"He had high ethical standards," she said. "He was a rare exemplar of what is best in character in his daily relations with his fellow men."

His friends described him as temperamental but sincere in his efforts. His critics couldn't find terms harsh enough to describe him. He was in more litigation than any other man in Johnstown. A number of cases listed him as the defendant in suits ranging from assault to defrauding people who took loans out from his bank.[33]

Cauffiel served as both mayor and chief magistrate. From the early nineteenth century until the mid-twentieth century, mayor's courts were a common feature in Pennsylvania and in the United States. Mayors were given the same powers as magistrates. Though it seemed to violate the separation of powers principle on the local level, chief executives of cities like Johnstown were entrusted with administrative powers of one office and adjudication powers of another. Cauffiel had such influence.

P. & A. Photos
MAYOR JOSEPH CAUFFIEL

Johnstown mayor Joseph Cauffiel appears in the *Minneapolis Star* in August 1922. Cauffiel was a well-known figure nationally for his antics, including legalizing the sale of alcohol for a period of time in an effort to draw in more Prohibition agents. *Newspapers.com.*

Early in his second term, he turned his executive wrath on a group of men and women while presiding over police court. When a group of black and white men came before him in January 1920 for various common crimes committed in the city, he declared vengeance upon them and sentenced them heavily. Behind the mayor on the wall was a flaming depiction of Lady Justice, blindfolded and armed with a sword. It was an unusual picture, the likeness of the famous goddess whose hand held aloft the scales of justice, as a local newspaper reporter put it. The sword seemed to be propped against her skirts, the hand that should be grasping it and arm being covered, with Old Glory in loose folds from one shoulder to her feet. With that as the backdrop, the mayor pressed and grilled defendants about the criminal underbelly of the city. He was never lenient with black men.

"Had the lash been laid upon their backs in a literal sense and the bleeding marks filled with salt, the unfortunates would not have cringed with more pain than when jail sentences were imposed and heavy fines exacted," a reporter wrote of the day's proceedings.

Cauffiel entertained people with his courtroom behavior. At best, his treatment of defendants was unorthodox. At worst, it was rash. One traveling salesman came before him in October 1920 for taking an eighteen-year-old girl to a Johnstown hotel room and keeping her there overnight. Cauffiel said that the man needed more than just a fine or sentence.

"What I ought to give you is a good body-beating instead of a fine of $100," Cauffiel said as he stood up and stepped close to the portly man. "Take him out of here before I do hit him."[34]

Cauffiel alternatingly used his executive and judicial authority to accomplish his goals. In December 1920, he invoked police power of startling magnitude and directed that four barrooms be closed at high noon. Officers guarded the entrances to the saloons to prevent people from coming in.[35] Cauffiel was heavy-handed in his penalties for violating the Volstead Act. He once compared selling whiskey to bartering in human traffic.[36] Defense attorneys accused Cauffiel of violating the Constitution insofar as property rights and due process in dealing with liquor sellers. Cauffiel described himself as a crusader against liquor peddlers throughout his tenure. The local white religious community supported him for his tough stance on booze.

Johnstown chief of police Charles Briney and Cauffiel were often at odds with each other. When the mayor said a vice crusade was on in the city in 1920, the chief quickly disputed the idea in the local newspapers.

"We are going to continue our enforcement of law and order just as we have endeavored to do in the past," Briney said. "We are short about 21 men on the police force and are not in position to engage in any special crusade. We do not think it is necessary. With our depleted force of officers we have been able to keep the city remarkably free of crime and vice."

Cauffiel had a bad reputation among

Joseph Cauffiel drew the ire of numerous publications across the country for his antics during the whole ordeal. He claimed that newspapers in Pittsburgh and New York City knew very little about the problems in Johnstown. *Public domain.*

the local media. In February 1922, he barred Herman Hassell, a *Johnstown Tribune* reporter, from police court hearings because he felt the journalist was biased or employed by one of Cauffiel's political rivals. The newspaper's managing editor, J. Campbell Murphy, went to city hall to protest the decision. The mayor accused Hassell of making misstatements and expressed his opinion that he was dishonest. Hassell came into the room to confront his accuser. Cauffiel responded by refusing to repeat the assertions and opened with a torrent of abuse directed against the editor and reporter. Murphy told Cauffiel that he should get a clean bill of health before he attacked other people. They almost came to fisticuffs, with Murphy attempting to punch Cauffiel in the face. An officer arrested Murphy and took him to Briney, who let the editor return to his newsroom. Hassell was allowed to leave city hall without being placed under arrest.

When contacted by the *Johnstown Democrat*, which wrote about the incident involving its rival newspaper, Cauffiel said, "This man Murphy came to my office in city hall today and with his first words proved he was entirely out

Joseph Cauffiel was one of the most outspoken members of the Republican Party in Johnstown. He had a private police force that he used to accomplish his political goals. As a person who served as both mayor and magistrate, he was one of the most powerful people in Johnstown at the time. *Public domain.*

of place, entirely out of his latitude. I was not minded to take much notice of the fellow, but suddenly he applied to me a name I'll take from no man. I had to summon all my self-control to keep from administering to him the punishment he deserved. I do not care to make a community issue out of J. Campbell Murphy's escapade by discussing him and his doings any further. Good night."

Cauffiel employed officers to work directly under him, without Briney's knowledge. When the issue was brought to city council's attention in 1922, Briney said he would not pay the officer in question for those duties since he was unaware of what his duties were. Cauffiel didn't tell the council or the chief what he employed the deputy and other officers to do. Cauffiel said that he intended to pay the cop and that he wasn't the only one on his private payroll.

The mayor and Briney had some tense exchanges during their mutual time in office. One, which involved a criminal case Cauffiel was embroiled in, went as such:

"Well, mayor, I'm better off than you. You're going to jail and I'm not," Briney said.

"If, in the end, I have to go to jail, I'm going to be pretty certain that others high in life go there to keep me company," Cauffiel responded.

One night in February 1922, Mayor Cauffiel canvassed the city trying to find 10 people in each ward to aid him in law enforcement. He planned to have a force of 210 citizens, 10 in each ward of the city, to aid him in the crusade. At the same hour he was lining up his forces, a truck driver and a constable, members of the so-called Cauffiel Detective Agency, were given a hearing before an alderman on charges of violating the liquor laws.

Cauffiel tried to catch cops drinking. After Cauffiel discovered that Briney drank alcohol at a party, he used it as a chance to get back at Briney. Cauffiel suspended the chief for ten days. Cauffiel held a hearing to prove his case against the chief. It was closed to the public, so the crowd at city hall was disappointed it couldn't hear more. Attorney Percy Allen Rose, who represented Briney, called the hearing a farce.

"You may state for me that the closed hearing was against my wishes," Rose said. "There was positively nothing developed at the hearing which the public might not well have heard. The mayor failed absolutely to substantiate the charges of conduct unbecoming a public official, and I deem it a gross injustice, and a man of Mr. Briney's high character shouldn't be humiliated by such farcical procedures as that of this morning."

The council exonerated Briney and rebuked Cauffiel.

In August 1922, at the height of Prohibition, Cauffiel, who supported Prohibition, was frustrated that federal agents wouldn't patrol the city for booze. His solution was to establish an elaborate hoax. He declared the city "wet" and permitted alcohol sales. Immediately, he was inundated with telegrams from across the country either applauding or denouncing him, and the state legislature threatened to impeach him. But his bet paid off. Prohibition agents flooded the city.

Around Johnstown, the order was seen as a publicity stunt, as it had taken place during the May primary in which George Wertz, who supported the sale of alcohol, had beaten Anderson Walters, a Prohibition supporter, for the Republican nomination for Congress. Wertz was a shoo-in, and Cauffiel thought that would result in lax enforcement of the Volstead Act.

A few months into 1923, Cauffiel electrified a Bible class audience with the promise that he would call out the United States Cavalry to chase rumrunners out of the county.

Cauffiel generally treated minorities and foreigners with disdain. Early in his second administration, Cauffiel staged an "execution" of a black man in police court when a police officer shot at him with blank cartridges. Cauffiel described it as "horseplay."

For the offense, the *Johnstown Tribune* raised the possibility of a trial for the mayor. Sentiment throughout the city seemed to be divided about the mayor, many believing that he had been sufficiently punished by the condemnation in the papers he had received for pushing the legal limit.

Cauffiel said the whole thing was overplayed in the local media.

"The press has made a great crime out of something that was neither authorized nor directed by me and I have sufficient proof to show that such is the case," he told the *Johnstown Democrat*. "This was no deadly weapon, but a simple, harmless toy gun. I am sorry for a few of the 'low brows.' They have created an unfavorable sentiment in Johnstown which is liable to break loose at any moment. I believe in fair play for every man who tries to be a man. I have tried to maintain order and enforce the laws of the commonwealth and the ordinances of the city and to protect the oath of office which I have taken to 'obey, protect and defend the constitution of the United States, the state of Pennsylvania and the laws of the land!' This I will do, not knowing either friend or foe in the protection of this obligation as well as my country. I ask the citizens of Johnstown to protect themselves."

Black leaders criticized Cauffiel for his treatment of their community. In March 1921, the Cambria A.M.E. Zion congregation passed a resolution attacking both Cauffiel's treatment of them in police court and his practice of jailing African Americans on suspicion.

Cauffiel made a number of public statements denouncing the importation of "undesirables," aimed at the black people moving in. He said recruiters collected the worst types of people from slums throughout the industrial centers in the North to come work in the city. He said many men came before him in police court and told him they were shipped in. Cauffiel told the newspaper that they were rejected by the local mills and had consequently taxed the resources of the community. He said it was an unjust imposition on the taxpayers of Cambria County and Johnstown. Cauffiel described them in criminal terms. Penn State professor Charles Lumpkins drew parallels between what Cauffiel's tactics were and the electoral strategy of many contemporary politicians.

"If a politician talks big about fighting crime, the politician, and I don't care what party, they'll say crime, crime, crime to strike fear in people," Dr. Lumpkins said. "Many people don't want to become victims. So they take it with caution. That's what they want to err on. Every demographic has its good people and bad people. The good people outnumber the bad people. But we can't control the bad people. That's what police are for."

Cauffiel's approach to court and governing discredited him among his peers. District Attorney D.P. Weimer said Cauffiel never held a legal police court. His distrust of others in public service didn't endear him either. Cauffiel hired special detectives to check on the loyalty of his own police force.

His term expired in January 1924. He was a candidate for reelection in the primary, which was to be held on September 18, 1923. He trailed behind the other candidates but hoped to catch up.

Cauffiel told people at great length the feeling he claimed existed against Bethlehem for bringing in Mexicans and black people. He directed most of his racism toward blacks, as he thought Mexicans were an afterthought. But he didn't distinguish. Cauffiel didn't understand black people and Mexicans living in Rosedale. He had never been there.

On the Monday after the shooting of the police officers in Rosedale, eight black people were arrested in Minersville for being disorderly and suspicious. They were charged with having made threatening remarks against Johnstown policemen after the Rosedale shootings while in a restaurant. Officers claimed the suspects discussed the shooting and remarked about "getting" some of the other men in uniform. Most of those rounded up had been in the city for a few months and had been shipped in to work. They had been in Johnstown for only a short time.

In police court, Cauffiel fined them various amounts and sentenced them to the jail in Ebensburg. One man was fined $100 or given the option of sixty days in the jail. Cauffiel then used the incarceration as pressure to make them leave Johnstown. Two days later, the mayor fined Levi Samuels for gambling. Samuels, who wrecked the car Young was in before the shooting, was in jail following the incident. Cauffiel imposed fines and ordered them to leave town. They agreed to go. Cauffiel was particularly terse with one of the defendants.

"Nigger, do you know what would happen to you down South?" he asked. "Well I'll tell you. They would take you out and hang you. You have fifteen minutes to leave Johnstown, one hour to leave the county, five hours to leave the state and seven hours to get below the Mason-Dixon line."

Cauffiel asked a number of black defendants similar questions. And he answered for them. In another exchange, he was just as intolerant.

"Where are you from?"

"Mississippi."

"Better have stayed there," Cauffiel said. "They know how to take care of you down there. You know, nigger, you'd be hanging from a tree in the South if you and your kind had killed three white policemen and just about killed three others."

"You start right back there. Ninety days in the county paid, or $100 and cost. Better pay your fine, nigger, and then get out of the state within five hours. If any of the policemen see you again you will be brought back here and you'll stay here from then on."

In any given court session, he addressed about half a dozen black defendants. On the day following the Rosedale shooting, he had 125 come before him. There were other magistrates in the area handling cases in the same fashion. The charges on the docket were "drunk," "suspicious," "possession of deadly weapons" and "disorderly conduct."

The first few days of September, quite a number of individuals were fined $100 and costs and, in default of the payment, were committed to the county jail in Ebensburg, which was about an hour north. Their terms of imprisonment ran from thirty to ninety days. In the hearings where he dismissed charges, Cauffiel told them he would "give them two hours to get out of town."

Some black people consulted local attorneys but generally they didn't have counsel. Ninety days in prison was the maximum time Cauffiel could dole out, and he gave that sentence frequently.

African Americans were not the only ones brought before court. During the same period, six Mexicans were arrested and were ordered out. The Mexicans did not seem to have angered the people of Johnstown as much as the black community had. But Cauffiel was cruel with both groups.

The black community in Johnstown feared the police during that time because they realized that if they were arrested Cauffiel would sentence them and subject them to harsh treatment. Word spread throughout Rosedale that Cauffiel was on a rampage. The tone Cauffiel set during those hearings encouraged many of the white supremacists in the area. The atmosphere grew more hostile with each passing day. And Cauffiel thought there was a political opportunity in all that anger.

KEEPING THE PEACE

Officers Otto Fink, William Bender and Joseph Grachan showed signs of improvement at the beginning of the next week, according to hospital reports. Fink was still listed as serious, but hospital staff said his condition had slightly improved.[37] The bullet remained in him, but if he continued to get better, they planned to make another effort to take it out of his back. Bender was in the same room as Fink. He had improved the most. Grachan would be subject to further operation to remove a bullet from his lung.

News that Captain Fink's condition had turned for the better quickly spread downtown and was the basis of the evening's conversation at police headquarters. Several officials of the department were admitted to the captain's room at Memorial Hospital. Later, officers said that Fink joked with them. Lieutenant Bender said he would have to shave pretty soon. The visitors reported that Fink had engaged in conversation and that his voice, while weak, did not falter. His outward condition impressed them as being favorable.

The hospital discharged Otto Nukem. He visited police headquarters with his arm in a sling, but his injury was expected to keep him from going to work for a while.

As for one of the deceased officers, James left behind a widow and five children. Hundreds visited the James residence on Somerset and Dibert Streets to view the body before the services took place.

Otto Fink, one of the officers who was killed during the shootout with Robert Young. *Officers Down Memorial Page, www.odmp.org.*

The Reverend C.C. Hays and the Reverend T.B. Dickson, of the First Presbyterian Church, officiated James's funeral. Both lauded the officer's work in the community. In their eulogy, the late county detective was described as a man who had "died in carrying out his duties."

James was referred to as a "fearless upholder of what he knew to be right."[38]

The reverends stressed his love of justice, fair play and the enforcement of law and order during the funeral services. They placed his body in the receiving vault at Grandview Cemetery to await the arrival of his sister from California.

Following a conference with city officials, Mayor Joseph Cauffiel issued an order prohibiting the sale of firearms to anyone by a pawnbroker or arms dealer within the limits of Johnstown. There had been a push by the newspapers for stricter gun laws. The *Johnstown Tribune* said that guns or other deadly weapons had become part of the usual wearing apparel for far too large a part of the population. Obtaining a revolver was too easy, with a score of stores handling firearms and ammunition with no restrictions. The guns, combined with alcohol and drugs, made every carrier a potential killer.

"Drugs and a gun—and the lives of brave men are sacrificed, families are desolated, a whole city is in mourning for the victims and is seething with resentment against conditions that will allow such things to happen," according to the *Tribune* editorial board.

They said every indication pointed to the fact that one man was responsible for the shooting. Not one scrap of evidence existed that anyone except Young was involved. The editorial then mentioned that Young was drug-crazed:

> *Somewhere is the man or men who supplied the drug, the men really responsible for the killings. Somewhere, waxing fat and wealthy on ill-gotten gains, is someone with the stain of murder on his soul. It is affairs such as these which bring to the surface the fact that there is a large trade in illicit drugs here, as in other cities.*

Every policeman knew it, the editorial said. There were drug fiends throughout the city. Occasionally, they ran amok. Occasionally, there was a tragedy, an arrest, a conviction, but the frightful traffic, as the editors put it, continued. Recreational drug use was most widespread among the criminals, where its sanity-ravaging effects were most dangerous. The newspaper's editors hoped that the police followed the drug peddlers' trails and brought them to justice. Guns were part of the usual ensemble in those troubled communities. The combination of drugs and guns worried everyone.

"The authorities are helpless," the *Tribune* said. "Anyone with the price can get a gun and there is no law which prevents such purchase. There is a law against the carrying of a concealed deadly weapon, but too often the first evidence of the carrying of a weapon is its use in the commission of a deadly crime."[39]

The *Tribune*'s editorial writer added that the police had done wonders while being understaffed. Efforts to enlarge the force were thwarted over the years.

"The peace of the city depends on the men who make up the police force," the editorial read. "The city has grown tremendously, and there have been many problems which, 20 years ago, were unknown here. Among those are the 'colonies,' such as Rosedale. The force is entirely too small to properly care for the territory under its jurisdiction. The pay is entirely too small for the service which the men render and for the responsibility they have. There is not a night during which a policeman does not take his life in his hands, for no one knows when a killer is going to break loose, or when a murderous burglar may be encountered."

One man alone should never cover police beats such as Rosedale, the paper asserted. Most other cities had two men patrolling an area at any one time. There weren't enough men in Johnstown.

"One of the tasks of the Mayor, who is the head of the police department, and Council, should be to work out the police problem here," the editorial continued. "With all due respect to the gentlemen involved, it might be well for them to consult with the executive officers of the police force and get the ideas of experts from other cities. Johnstown is a city of metropolitan status, and 'small town' methods should be cast into the discard. Police officials, here and in other cities, have made a study of methods, and there is no reason why Johnstown should not reap the benefits of these studies."

State troopers from Greensburg remained on duty in Rosedale. City police officers also patrolled the vicinity. People visited the scene in their cars. Garrulous residents of Rosedale who claimed to have witnessed it all refought the shooting. Little credence was placed in any of the stories, inasmuch as police believed that there was no one observer who witnessed the continuous movements of Young and the police officers.

Although several black men were still held on suspicion, nothing new was expected to be uncovered in the case through their questioning. Nine black people arrested at Rosedale by local officers and state police were given a hearing.

Cauffiel continued his efforts to rid the city of black criminals. Carl Williams, arrested on suspicion of an undisclosed crime, was fined $100 and costs. James Mossell was given a similar fine when a knife was found in his possession. James D. Rose also had a knife, and he was given the same penalty. Alternative sentences of ninety days in the county jail were given out in three cases. Cauffiel ordered Thomas Ferguson, Lewis Nickelow,

Thomas Horsey and John Wilson out of town for similar crimes. They promised to leave.

The usual curious crowd gathered about city hall and the city patrol, and the alley at the rear of the side of the police station had to be cleared several times.

A group of black men and women issued a statement to the *Johnstown Democrat*:

> *We the Negro citizens whose forefathers were among the pioneer settlers here, deeply regret the tragic disturbance which occurred in Rosedale Thursday evening. We are sorry indeed that such an element does exist in our city, as never before in the history of Johnstown have we found such conditions.*
>
> *Our police stand as intrepid mediators between the citizens and crime and should be respected and honored as such. We furthermore, out of profound heartfelt sympathy, collectively and individually, offer condolence to the bereaved families and friends. We further suggest that such characters as Young be not permitted to enter our city and that through municipal and legal enactments that dens of dissipation and sources of crime be abolished. We greatly commend Officer Yoder for his successful capture of the outlaw.*

The trustees, members and friends of Cambria A.M.E. Zion Church wrote a letter that commented on the trouble. The pastor and church officers signed it.

"The respectable colored people of our community are not in sympathy with this act and as law-abiding citizens we do not tolerate such actions," the statement read. "We ask that the city and county authorities put forth every effort to close the places of vice, dissipation and the sources from which the questionable Negroes secure their drugs, in this we assure you of our cooperation. We also extend our sympathy to the bereaved families and the unfortunate ones."

Black employees from the Lorain Steel Company, a factory that produced trolley rails and systems that was located in the Moxham neighborhood of the city, wrote a letter to white residents. It appeared in the *Johnstown Tribune*:

> *We, as law abiding colored people residing in Johnstown, wish to inform all citizens that we sincerely regret the unfortunate shooting affray which occurred in Rosedale last Thursday evening for which a misguided member of our race was responsible. The individual who caused the deaths and wounding of the officers who were arresting him has paid the penalty for*

his rash act. We stand ready to aid the authorities on such occasions to maintain law and order in this community. We do not subscribe to such an outrage as was committed last week in Rosedale.

They went on to be magnanimous to white residents:

We realize the white people of America are the best friends of the Negro. We desire that such a feeling of mutual respect may continue to exist in this city and that law-abiding colored people may not be generally condemned for the act of a citizen of this race.

The *Johnstown Tribune* said the city was to be congratulated on its self-control:

There were mutterings here and there from hotheads; threats of "vengeance" were made; an undercurrent of feeling was noticeable, feeling which was wrongly directed at the race to which the murderer belonged. It would have been a catastrophe if any mob action had been taken. Any such movement would have inevitably resulted in more killings; more bereaved homes; more frightfulness. And it was not worth the cost.

The paper added that there was mob spirit aroused throughout the country. But Johnstown wasn't susceptible to it, according to the newspaper:

It is utterly unjust to condemn and punish all members of any race for the crimes and shortcomings of individual members of it. Admitted that there are lawbreakers, bad men, potential murderers in any one race, it is un-American to visit on all the punishment for the crimes of a few. Johnstown for many years has had Negro citizens of sterling worth. Many of them have, in their humble way, achieved the respect, confidence and liking of the city at large. To miss these, and the decent ones among the newcomers, with the riff-raff is unjust; to punish them for the crimes of others is unthinkable.

THE ORDER

Cauffiel called the *Johnstown Democrat* newsroom a week after the shooting and told the city editor that he wanted to give them an exclusive. The editor assigned Ray Krimm to the story. Krimm and his editor were suspicious as to why a Republican mayor wished the article to be printed exclusively in the Democratic paper, but because the Republican paper didn't support Cauffiel for renomination, they played along.[40]

Cauffiel told Krimm that, until further orders, black people in Johnstown were prohibited from holding public gatherings and couldn't assemble except for church. Picnics, public and private dances and similar events weren't permitted.

He said black people who recently came to Johnstown should clear out and that there would be a ban on future migration to the community. Cauffiel said he would take immediate steps to compel every black person visiting Johnstown to register and report to either the mayor or chief of police. No black person would be allowed within Johnstown unless it was proved beyond a doubt that he or she was law-abiding. Black people visiting Johnstown were required to report their whereabouts and give a complete record of their business or social activities while within the city. Cauffiel thought that would keep criminals out.

"Native Negroes will be requested to take their guest or guests to the chief of police immediately upon the stranger's arrival in Johnstown," he said. "They must give assurance that the visitor is of good character and that he is a law-abiding citizen. We shall also report, in fact, I demand, that strangers report to police headquarters or to me at the end of every week they remain in Johnstown. They will be asked to give a complete record of what they have been doing during the week."

Cauffiel appealed to white citizens, but he also reached out to the entrenched black population that had been present before the Great Migration.

"They want to do what is right," Cauffiel said. "I am convinced that they are as ashamed of the Rosedale occurrence as anybody can be. They want to do their share in upholding law and order. Here is their chance to cooperate with us fully."

Cauffiel contended that 1,500 to 2,000 black people had left Johnstown that week. Unsaid was that he had been bringing them before court en masse and threatening them with hefty fines and lengthy prison sentences. In explaining his drastic order, he said he was obligated to do it.

"This act, I feel, is my personal duty for the place and protection of our law-abiding citizens and the good of our city. Our old native Negroes will stand by me on this issue," he asserted. "They have always been law-abiding citizens, and they can help us suppress this recent outbreak of lawlessness. I ask that all good citizens take into consideration the good record of our native Negroes. They should not be molested. The crowd we are after is that riff-raff that has been shipped in on us. I feel the old native Negroes will give us aid to abolish this lawlessness."

Cauffiel ordered the immediate removal from Johnstown of every black person who had not been a local resident for more than seven years. He took drastic steps to clear the city of them. According to later reports, some were marched out at gunpoint.

"I want every Negro who has lived here less than seven years to pack up his belongings and get out," the mayor told the newspaper. He added that he wanted the removal "carried out at once."

He continued to target the migrants.

"We cannot tell how many of these Negroes who have been shipped in here have criminal records," Cauffiel complained, "until we get them in some escapade or act of lawlessness and then write back to their hometown to secure their records. Such procedure has cost the city of Johnstown the lives of two of her most faithful police officers and has placed four others in local hospitals, two of the wounded yet being in serious conditions, with their prospects of living yet undetermined."

Cauffiel told Krimm that he gave the order a great deal of consideration: "I have gone over this thing carefully. This is not a hasty decision for me to give out. I have worked over our Negro problem in Johnstown and have kept on the job night and day during the last week trying to work out a solution. My mind is made up. The Negroes must go back from where they came. They are not wanted in Johnstown."

As the mayor gave the interview, the telephone on his desk jangled. It was a man asking for permission to hold a dance for black people in the eleventh ward. The answer was an emphatic no.

"Tell them for me," the mayor said turning from the telephone, "that this ban on Negroes congregating for any purpose whatsoever other than church is in effect right this very minute and that it will remain in effect until we can see our way clear to lift it. There will be no special privileges and none need ask for them. The same order applies throughout Johnstown."

Concluding his interview, Cauffiel said the plans and order he made public were for the welfare of the people. He felt confident that the "right" element of people within the city would back his plans on what he termed the "Negro problem." He expected cooperation in driving the undesirable element from Johnstown's gates.

The headline stood out from the rest of the others on the September 7, 1923, front page of the local section of the *Johnstown Democrat*. In large, bold and italicized lettering, it said:

Mayor Cauffiel Says Undesirable Negroes Must Quit Johnstown

The sub-headline read, "Says only those who have been here seven years will be permitted to remain and that future importations will be barred—admits, however, that some new arrivals make good citizens and speaks highly of older residents of that race."[41]

BURNING INTOLERANCE

The flaming crosses of the Ku Klux Klan pierced a foggy sky the night after the article was published, as hundreds of local members of the order staged gigantic demonstrations in twelve sections of the city simultaneously. From every hill and mountainside, on all sides of the city, crosses blazed. At the height of the demonstration, the *Johnstown Democrat* received a telephone call from a Klansman.

"We want you to understand that our demonstration tonight is not directed toward the law-abiding Negroes of Johnstown," he said. "We are after that dirty crew that has been sent into Johnstown—those questionable characters gathered from questionable neighborhoods in other cities and dumped upon Johnstown to stage their drunken revels, their shooting sprees and their murderous designs. It is to that class of the Negro race that we are directing our forces. They may take our demonstration tonight as a warning. They are not wanted in Johnstown. Tell them to clear out."

Before hanging up, the Klansman said that law-abiding black citizens of Johnstown had nothing to fear.

"It is that band of murderers we are after," the speaker said.

Asked whether the local Klan approved of Mayor Cauffiel's order, the Klansman said that they were heartily in favor of it.

The Ku Klux Klan always took advantage of such opportunities to grow memberships. Clarke and Tyler gave autonomy to local Klaverns. Decentralizing the message attracted initiates by exploiting local grievances and by appeasing local elites. A Klan manual of leadership told readers that they must know completely what is wrong with each community. At the moment, the biggest issue on everyone's minds was the racial tension gripping the city. People feared a riot. They were angry that policemen died, and the Klan decided to exploit that situation.

After cross burnings, Klan recruiters distributed pamphlets discussing their principles. One of the pamphlets was *Ideals of the Ku Klux Klan*, which said the organization stood for white supremacy. It explained their dedication to patriotism, the Constitution, the flag and the public school system.

"Every effort to wrest from White Men the management of [the nation's] affairs in order to transfer it to the control of blacks or any other color, or permit them to share in its control, is an invasion of our sacred constitutional prerogatives and a violation of divinely established laws," it read. "Every effort to wrest from the White Man control of this country must be resisted.… We would not rob the colored population of their rights, but we demand that they respect the rights of the White Race in whose country they are permitted to reside. When it comes to the point that they cannot and will not respect those rights, they must be reminded that this is a White Man's country, so they will seek for themselves a country more agreeable to their tastes and aspirations."

While the Klan thought it had universal support, some prominent white religious leaders spoke against the organization after the shooting and cross burnings. The Reverend C.C. Hays of the First Presbyterian Church was one of the Klan's critics.

"We are being put to the test as to our ability to govern ourselves and the multiplicity of organizations such as the Ku Klux Klan, which propose to take the law into their own hands, is not helping the situation any," he said in a sermon. "Two wrongs will never make a right. Justice must be open and above board or it is not justice."

Other racially charged incidents happened shortly following the order. Timely intervention by steel company police prevented a near riot and a mob assault upon Samuel Haskins, a black employee of the Bethlehem Steel Company at the Franklin open-hearth plant, after Haskins was alleged to have choked a white coworker at the plant. Haskins was logged into the Franklin jail after he fled from a mob of workmen who witnessed the assault. They chased after him while throwing hard objects. He took refuge in the watchman's office at the plant gate while the mob waited outside.

Attention was still focused on the officers' well-being. The Colt-Alber Chautauqua Company, under the auspices of the Pythian Temple Association, held a program that raised money for the police relief fund.

Admission was free for the show, but a silver offering was taken. The Dunbar Quartet and Hand Bell Ringers performed.

Officers sold a large number of benefit tickets at a Knights of Columbus Circus and Festival at the Woodvale grounds. There were twenty-one booths stocked with novelty items. It was so well supported by the public that the hundreds of admission tickets given to policemen when they reported at roll call at 6:00 p.m. were gone two hours later, with police in all sections of the city calling into city hall for extra supplies. It was impossible to meet the demand. More were printed in the morning. Thousands of people came. It was later announced on the last night of the festival that all money collected at the event would go to the police fund. Everything that wasn't sold would be put up for auction, with the proceeds going to the wounded officers.[42]

Hospital staff regarded Captain Otto Fink's condition as extremely serious. He was delirious, and the attending physician at the hospital sent pessimistic messages to the public. A surgeon removed the bullet that lodged into his back. They hoped that his unusually strong physique would help him recover. Marie Sutton, nurse in attendance, cared for Fink. The other wounded men recuperated. Officer Joseph Grachan, with a bullet wound in his right lung, was getting better. Grachan's condition was reported as "greatly improved."

Before that, nurses told newspaper reporters that he was probably going to die. The officer rallied during the days following his hospital admission. While unable to predict his recovery until further developments, Mercy Hospital nurses said that Grachan "might pull through" and that his chances were good.

No one told Fink of the deaths of Detective James or Abrahams. Among the visitors to Memorial Hospital were Mayor Cauffiel and Chief of Police Briney.[43]

Two weeks to the day after the sensational shooting, City Detective Otto Nukem died of heart trouble at the home of his parents in Listonburg in Somerset County while at the breakfast table. Nukem was at his parents' house because of his mother's illness and planned to return to Johnstown. Nukem had been in ill health for a year, following a bout of influenza. He had recovered from the wound nicely, though he had not returned to work. The forty-six-year-old Somerset County native left behind a widow, Mary Nukem, and two daughters, Vera and Mary Elizabeth Nukem.[44]

Mayor Cauffiel went about his business as if nothing extraordinary happened. He suggested to city council members that they supply Johnstown's police department with tear bombs, hand grenades and other equipment for combatting mob violence. The mayor offered a number of suggestions that he said might be carried out if the police were confronted with another situation like the Rosedale shooting.

The shooting was up for extended discussion during the council meeting. The council, as a body, formally thanked the citizens of Johnstown for their contributions to the relief fund. Councilman Thomas J. Harris suggested that the body appropriate an emergency relief fund to tide over the families until the council received state appropriation funds from the city's insurance. Harris recommended that council pass a resolution calling upon other third-class cities through Pennsylvania to

Otto Nukem, another officer who eventually died because of the shootout. *Officers Down Memorial Page, www.odmp.org.*

cooperate in having state legislation enacted allowing municipalities to create emergency funds such as those for the Rosedale situation. Harris criticized the red tape that had to be untangled to get the relief money.

Briney, who headed an understaffed police force that lost officers frequently to the higher-paying mills, publicly came off as the voice of reason throughout much of the Rosedale affair. He stated that the shooting was the action of one man. He issued patrols to quell the mobs from attacking black residents. And unlike Cauffiel, he was on a talking basis with many black leaders in Johnstown. But the police force, during the Rosedale affair, rounded up black people on suspicion and charged them with crimes. Whether they were under the direction of Cauffiel or Briney is unclear. But it allowed Cauffiel to enforce his order when the African Americans and Mexicans came to police court.

Briney wasn't alone in holding a low opinion of Cauffiel. D.P. Weimer, a Republican, had been a commissioner before taking office as a district attorney in 1915. He also had a private law practice in Johnstown. Weimer and Cauffiel didn't like each other for much of the same reason Cauffiel didn't like anyone—Weimer didn't support the Volstead Act. Weimer was no friend to the Klan, as he would later be involved in prosecutions against some of its members.

Despite his disdain for Cauffiel, Weimer didn't run police court. For many of the black residents in Rosedale and elsewhere in Johnstown,

Cauffiel's order was seen as enforceable because of his position as magistrate. Cauffiel's words were taken seriously given that prison and heavy fines were very real possibilities and seemed to be doled out with much greater frequency than before the shooting.

By and large, the public seemed to approve, according to an article in the *Philadelphia Public Ledger*. County authorities hadn't acted and said that so long as order was maintained, they wouldn't interfere, according to the newspaper.

THE GOOD DEMOCRAT

In the days after the order, the *Johnstown Democrat* published an editorial chastising the mayor.

"The good mayor again steps into the limelight with an order expelling every Negro from the community who has not lived here seven years or longer," it said. "This order is likely to attract almost as much attention as his famous 'good beer' edict. It will appeal in particular to Ku Kluxers and other folks who cherish race prejudice. Doubtless many perfectly well-meaning people will applaud the mayor and some of them may fancy that he possesses authority to banish all who do not come up to some arbitrary standard of color or length of residence or degree of desirability."

The *Democrat* said that crazed white men committed crimes as deadly as Young's, but that guilt was not prescribed to all white men afterward. "It happens that black men in this country are free American citizens. Their rights are precisely equal to those of white citizens. They are as free to come and go in seeking employment and in trying to better their condition. It would appear that the mayor has not a legal leg to stand on in putting out this extraordinary ban."

The editorial board claimed Cauffiel issued the order for political gain: "The capitalization of these hatreds and prejudices for political purpose has been common in other parts of the country and it is not inconceivable that there are those in our midst who would capitalize them if they could. But in doing so they would be playing with fire. About this there should be no doubt."

To their credit, the *Johnstown Tribune*'s editors didn't want to give Cauffiel the ink for fear of giving him the edge in his reelection efforts, according to the statewide investigation conducted later on into the incident. But Cauffiel's order appalled Warren Worth Bailey, the editor of the *Johnstown Democrat*. Bailey informed the American Civil Liberties Union about it.

Newspapers in cities as far away as Dallas gave Cauffiel unsparing attention. By 1923, racial animosity had reached its apex. That newspapers in the South condemned what took place in Pennsylvania was a sign that the nation was gradually emerging from one of the darkest and most intolerant periods of American history. At the same time that the Klan's membership peaked, a segment of society awakened to the evils of racism.

Cauffiel disparaged the national publications and cast their reporters as a misunderstanding group of outsiders unaware of the problems besetting his community. He told reporters that he acted in good faith.

"We have been sitting on a bomb in this city," Cauffiel said, "and it almost exploded last week when two of our policemen were killed and four others so badly wounded that one of them has since died and two others were so dangerously hurt their deaths may be expected at any time. This was done by a Negro who had quarreled with his wife.

"I was away, and when I came home and found the city in a ferment I decided that the only thing to do was send these newcomers out of town and keep them out. Resentment was running high. No less than a dozen flaming crosses were burned on the hilltops around the city and I feared an outbreak against the Negroes unless I acted promptly. I swore in a lot of extra policemen, arranged to have state police come in on short notice and then began disarming Negroes."

Cauffiel said the old black population was fine, but many of the newcomers were "bad people," including ex-convicts.

"I have no objection to the Negro because he is a Negro," the mayor deflected. "But the situation was such that we had to act quickly."

Within a day of Cauffiel's order, about three to four hundred more black residents either left the city or were prepared to leave, local police reported. City hall portrayed the order as being well received, even among some of the black population.

"In Johnstown's Negro settlements yesterday, the mayor's order was the one topic discussed. Among the native Negroes, who are allowed to remain if they have been residents of Johnstown for seven years or more, the order is said to have received endorsement, and the older Negroes, many of whom are descendants of the first Negro families to settle in the Conemaugh

THE COLD NORTH WIND

—Knott in the Dallas *News.*

A political cartoon that ran in the *Dallas Morning News* showed what much of the country thought of what transpired in Johnstown after Joseph Cauffiel ordered African American residents to leave the community if they had lived there less than seven years. *Courtesy of the Johnstown Area Heritage Association.*

Valley, were ready to give their cooperation in seeing that the mayor's order is carried out," public officials told the newspaper. But the statement came from political operatives working for Cauffiel. The misrepresentation of the incident by other people in the political establishment shows that the injustice was possible because many enabled Cauffiel to carry it out.

Mrs. James Whitehead reflected on the days of September 1923 to the *Tribune-Democrat* years later. "People turned mean then to blacks and said things like, 'If you don't move, we'll put you in jail.' This was when a lot of black families left," she said. "They were scared. They'd throw their belongings into a sheet and get out of town the best way they could."

Jesse Flagg, of Prospect, was in the community when it happened. He came back to Johnstown two days after the officers died. "Policemen picked me up at the railroad station and walked me over to the police station, where they searched my luggage to make sure I had no weapons," Flagg told the *Tribune-Democrat*. "Every colored person came in, they'd search his bags. They were running colored people out of town."

Flagg said Johnstown had been good in many ways up to that time. "You could get served in almost any restaurant," he said. "It didn't make much difference if you were colored. People treated you pretty nice. But after the shootings there was a lot of trouble."

Joe Davis, a porter and World War I veteran, was working at Levy's, a store in Johnstown, when the newspaper published Cauffiel's interview. He remembered, years later, some of the black people coming in, with fear in their eyes, to buy pistols and other weapons for protection. City detectives stood across the street and arrested some of the black people when they came out of the store.

"The detectives would watch through the windows and arrest the colored boys when they left the store," Davis said later. "My boss, Mr. Levy, protected them though. He never let them take the gun with them after they bought it. The gun would be delivered later."

Although black people bought guns for self-defense, there is no proof that they used any. The police arrested African Americans all over Rosedale, but they left Davis alone.

"They knew me," he said.

The entrenched African American community in Johnstown was equally as horrified by the order and as troubled by the inability to hold social events. Longtime black residents told the *Democrat* that they objected to the withdrawal of privileges to hold gatherings except church services. Some even went so far as to retain an attorney to fight the order.

Though Cauffiel acknowledged black people had a history and place, he didn't address the problem of how police officers or his supporters could differentiate between longtime black residents and those who had come within the period of time specified by the order. And since most of the African American population had come between 1916 and 1923, the majority of black people in Johnstown were affected by it.

Cauffiel ordered the police to search black homes for weapons, guns, hammers and kitchen knives. Officers on duty reported to Chief of Police Charles E. Briney that they noticed hasty preparations that forecast the immediate departure by many African Americans. The word of the mayor's order traveled quickly, and before noon people in every black residence were discussing it.

Cauffiel told a reporter for the *New York Call* the same thing he told Krimm: "The Negroes must go back to where they started. If they came from down south, well, tell 'em to get back over that Mason-Dixon Line and lose no time about it. I want every Negro and Negro family that hasn't been here seven years to clear out. Not only that, I want them to clear out at once. They are not wanted in Johnstown."

The *Democrat* estimated that two thousand black people left the city, attributing the number to police. One figure showed that between seven and eight hundred who came to Johnstown for work had picked up and left the city in one night—Friday, August 31—the night after the Rosedale incident. Perhaps they had foreseen what was to come.

TAKING NOTICE

About two and a half hours west of Johnstown was the newsroom of the *Pittsburgh Courier*, one of the country's leading black newspapers. Established in 1907, it gained national prominence after Robert Lee Vann became the editor, publisher, treasurer and legal counsel in 1910. It eventually grew to a circulation of 250,000, with more than 400 employees in fourteen cities. The *Courier* sought to empower black people through advocating for economic and political equality. Vann was its driving force.

Vann, originally from North Carolina, attended Western University of Pennsylvania in Pittsburgh and graduated from its law school in June 1909. He initially was the counsel for the *Courier*, which was founded by a small group of African Americans. When he took over, the paper rose in popularity in large part because of its stance against the poor treatment of black soldiers during World War I. Vann was also politically powerful, having served as the national director of "Negro" publicity in the Republican presidential campaign of Warren Harding in 1920.[45]

"He was an icon in western Pennsylvania because of the *Courier*," said Samuel W. Black of the Heinz History Center. "He was the face of the *Courier* up to his death. It meant a lot. It gave him a great deal of authority and influence nationwide as the *Courier* grew."

Vann, a handsome, well-dressed forty-four-year-old at the time, was determined. Employees noticed him working far into the evening without

As the editor of the Pittsburg Courier, one of the largest Negro newspapers in the world, Vann wielded a decisive influence for the welfare and progress of American Negroes and the American people.

ROBERT LEE VANN
LAWYER, EDITOR, CRUSADER.

In recognition of his contributions as journalist, public servant, and jurist, the Maritime Commission is naming a merchant man of its liberty fleet in his honor.

When the tower of the Belgian Pavilion at the World's Fair was presented to his alma mater, Virginia Union, it was renamed "The Robert Lee Vann Tower," as a tribute to his ardent interest and philanthropies in the field of education.

Robert Vann was one of the most respected newspapermen in the country regardless of race. His newspaper, the *Pittsburgh Courier*, shaped public sentiment within the black community nationwide. The Office for Emergency Management, which was a subset of the Office of War Information, created this drawing during World War II. *National Archives.*

stopping for dinner. Like thousands of other African Americans, he arrived in the North at the turn of the century, attracted by Pittsburgh's booming industry. But when he came, he saw the prejudice and discrimination that black men and women encountered.

Vann was vocal about things he disagreed with, and he used the newspaper as a platform to advocate for the things he cared about. He encouraged both whites and blacks to support the NAACP, among other organizations. The *Courier* touched on all aspects of black life, including housing, education, crime, employment and misrepresentation in the white press. Pittsburgh had a real need for an African American publication in the early part of the twentieth century, when most news of black people in local papers consisted of sensational criminal cases or lurid details such as quarrels between lovers and substance abuse.

"There was a use of the black press that went beyond just covering news of the day," Black said. "It became a link to progress. A link to knowing the oppression. And a link to connecting your own locale with the rest of the world. It was a window into the country and the world. I don't know if Hearst or if any of the other newspaper moguls had that kind of focus for their newspapers. But most African-American press did. They saw that there was a real need for their service."

Dr. William G. Jordan, author of *Black Newspapers & America's War for Democracy, 1914–1920*, noted that newspapers like the *Pittsburgh Courier* sought to end injustices.

"That was their goal," Jordan said. "The papers would report news from the black community. They would do feature stories on black businesses or people who were successful. It would print news from that perspective because the white press would ignore the black community or portray it in a negative light with crime. Partly they saw their role as bolstering black self-regard."

Its crusades often extended into less tangible, but psychologically important, facets of black life that had to improve for blacks to have a feeling of worth and racial pride and a sense of community. So Vann tried to stress black achievement and to create bonds among his readers.

"The white newspapers in those days even ran advertisements for jobs and for houses and apartments where they were permitted to put white only on those," Dr. Ralph Proctor said. "We felt minimized by white newspapers, but empowered by black newspapers. We knew what was going on. We knew what was going on from the perspective of black people as well."

Vann particularly blamed the *Pittsburgh Press* for inciting unrest through biased writing. And the newspaper left out many of the important details and events that had happened in the community. Any new developments to stories it had covered often went unpublished.

White newspapers in Pittsburgh like the *Post-Gazette*, *Sun-Telegraph* and *Pittsburgh Press* didn't publish information about African American marriages, deaths and births.

"They simply didn't cover anything of importance in the black community," Dr. Proctor said. "The only things in the black community they covered were the crime, the musicians and the athletes. The *Courier* was our eye on the world. The *Courier* told us what was going on and what was happening in our community. It was the advocate for black folks not only in Pittsburgh, but in the world."

Initially, the *Courier* misreported the Rosedale incident as a race riot. But it was not alone in that. The *Pittsburgh Press* reported that officers were attacked by a group of black men when they were sent to arrest a black man who had shot another cop. The *Press* alleged that Young's shooting attracted a crowd to the scene and more guns were fired as a result. This was the prevailing narrative due to the coverage white newspapers gave.

Other newspapers also misreported the Rosedale affray. The *Journal News*, in Hamilton, Ohio, reported that police officers initially came to Rosedale on a riot call. The paper said the incident grew out of a quarrel among the black residents and claimed the officers' assailants had escaped to nearby hills. The Ohio journal had picked up the report from the Associated Press. Many other newspapers carried the same story. The United Press, the other wire service in the country, also had a report that stated riot guns had been issued and several posses were scouring the county for others involved in the crime. The *Altoona Mirror* falsely reported that two black shooters had been at the scene. The second gunman, whose name was not known, could have been trying to assist police, they wrote.

But Vann and his newsroom soon got to the bottom of it. Vann improved the *Courier* during the 1920s with the additions he made to the staff. He was able to hire a number of capable people drawn from the growing ranks of black newspapers. In the postwar period, with the rise of the black press and black pride, journalism was beginning to attract talented young African American men and women who wished to become full-time reporters and editors. And if something unjust happened, they were quick to write about it.

"People who could write who were black couldn't get a job with white newspapers. So they had to write for *The Pittsburgh Courier*," Dr. Proctor noted. "So the very best writers who were black worked for *The Pittsburgh Courier* because they couldn't work elsewhere. You had to work where they could hire you. Nobody hired you everywhere else."

When news from Johnstown reached their offices, Vann and the staff of the *Courier* swung into action. Reporters were sent to the scene. Editorials condemned Cauffiel. And attention from national leaders focused on a mill town in western Pennsylvania. Thus was the power of the *Pittsburgh Courier* and the black press across America, which would become dedicated to providing an accurate account of what happened since the shooting. They portrayed Cauffiel as a tyrannical figure who had to be fought and overruled.

The news reached New York City shortly thereafter. Chandler Owen, the editor of the *Messenger Magazine*, a black-run publication, described Cauffiel as a Russian czar and offered in eviscerating words what he and the national African American community thought of him and his order. Owen took a lot of other newspapers to task for their coverage.

Owen and A. Philip Randolph, who later created the March on Washington movement, ran the *Messenger*. Dr. Jordan said that the *Messenger* was far more out of the mainstream than the *Pittsburgh Courier* and the *Chicago Defender*.

Chandler Owen, writer, editor and founder of the *Messenger,* a left-wing publication based out of Harlem, was one of the most eloquent and impassioned writers within the national black journalism community. Later in his life, he became disenchanted with socialism and began writing speeches for Republican candidates, including President Dwight Eisenhower. *Library of Congress, Prints and Photographs Division, Washington, D.C.*

"Those guys were socialists. It was considered a socialist publication," Jordan said. "That got banned from the mail during World War I. Those guys were critical of discrimination of African-Americans during the war."

The *Messenger* was based in Harlem, the epicenter of black culture at the time. The publication produced political commentary, literature of the "New Negro Movement" and harsh criticisms of world and national leaders for hypocrisy on racial matters. It opposed World War I and applauded the Bolshevik Revolution in Russia. It demanded government action to ensure civil liberties and protection and guarantee absolute social equality, including intermarriage and the rights of African Americans to arm themselves in self-defense. After the war ended, the U.S. Department of Justice created the General Intelligence Division, which was a precursor to the FBI. A twenty-four-year-old J. Edgar Hoover was put in charge of it. One of the groups Hoover targeted to investigate were journalists, including those who worked for the *Messenger.* Hoover viewed black journals and newspapers with suspicion. He thought they encouraged rioting and racial unrest. The federal government went after Owen for his political diatribes, and he was imprisoned because of some of the things he wrote. During the Johnstown incident, he was one of the most outspoken writers.

"You know anything about the Rosedale affair?" Owen asked his readers. "Well let us tell you. The 'white' papers report that a riot call went out for the police."

Owen then relayed the story given by other publications: One black man was crazed with moonshine, yet about twenty or more black people were barricaded in a building from which they veritably ambushed the police as soon as their cars drove up.

"Remember this is the report of the white papers, WE DO NOT BELIEVE IT," he wrote. "There's a screw loose somewhere. We had hoped the Pittsburgh papers would have dispatched representatives on the field and gotten the truth. It is preposterous that thirty Negroes would lurk in hiding and fire instantly upon policemen because they were coming to arrest a drunken Negro. Drunken Negroes, as well as whites, are arrested daily without a passing notice."

Owen told his readers about Cauffiel's order and prohibition on social gatherings. He then offered advice to African Americans who remained.

"Now a word to the Negroes of Johnstown," Owen wrote. "First, you don't have to go anywhere and no Negro with a spark of manhood, a scintilla of courage or an iota of brains is going to leave. It makes no difference whether you have been to Johnstown seven years, seven months, seven weeks, seven days or seven hours, your rights to remain are equal with those who have been there seventy years."

Owen told the Johnstown black population to hold dances and picnics when ready. He said to have them without seeking permission unless they were using public grounds and needed to get a permit. Owen said a man's home was his castle. He also told them that they did not need to register or report to the mayor or chief of police.

"It is nobody's business what you do unless you do something unlawful," he wrote. "If you desire to go to Johnstown, go ahead! If you desire to go to Johnstown to visit friends, go ahead! If you don't know a soul in Johnstown and would like to visit the city to look around, go ahead to Johnstown!"

Owen reaffirmed their rights: "We know just what the law is and what the rights of Negroes are and we propose to advise them and encourage them to utilize every right. The idea that a little peanut politician mayor of a Pennsylvania town can issue edicts and laws like a czar for Negroes to obey—is mere Tommyrot."

And he gave a final word on Cauffiel: "It stamps him, personally a resident of more than seven years, as about the most unlawful and unlaw-abiding resident of Johnstown."

NATIONAL FUROR

The *New York Times* sent a reporter to Johnstown to find out more about what was a national sensation in the week following the publication of Cauffiel's order. In a September 14 story, the *Times* reported that more than two thousand African Americans and Mexicans left the city, a large number were in jail and others were about to depart. Rosedale, where more than three thousand blacks and Mexicans had lived in bunkhouses, was basically deserted. Though other city officials believed that the mayor had no authority to give the order, they took no action to check the exodus. Intense feeling against the African American community continued throughout the city. Other leaders believed the mayor had widespread popular support for his move, though residents wearied of the national criticism.

Semiofficial figures from the Bethlehem Company, which employed the largest number of African Americans in Johnstown, showed that more than two thousand black and Mexican laborers had been paid off. The company was seriously handicapped and unable to find white replacements. It didn't protest to city officials, however.

Some lobbied Pennsylvania governor Gifford Pinchot to act. Lewis B. Moore, an investment broker in Philadelphia, wrote the governor on September 14. He commended Pinchot on his handling of the recent coal strike and then proceeded to discuss what happened in Johnstown.

Moore said that there was an absence of an interracial relations commission in Pennsylvania, which had been helpful in other states in acclimating black people to new areas. Moore said they would find more hospitable living arrangements and be more productive if a commission existed. He wanted to know the number of black people coming from the South, why they were coming and where they were going, how they were articulating into the communities they came to and what agencies could help them adjust.

"Such information placed before you governor, might not only be useful, but also might further aid you in adjusting national difficulties and pointing a way to other states as to how they may deal with Negro migrants in absorbing them into our community life without friction and make them a helpful asset rather than a civic liability."

Rose W. Wilson, president of the Women's Civic League, also sent a letter to the governor. "We the members of the women's civic league of America representing thousands of women of our race regret that it is necessary for us to register our protest against the unmanly attitude and the un-American utterances of the Mayor of Johnstown Joseph Cauffiel to the effect that the colored residents who had not lived there for the past seven years or more should leave town at once. We trust that every possible means of protection shall be assured to our groups and that his Excellency the governor will do all things in his power to exercise the power of his office to emulate this unpleasant episode."

Other major newspapers and news outlets took note. The *Harrisburg Telegraph* lambasted him. The *Nation*, a publication that covered hard news and politics, described Cauffiel as temperamental. The *Boston Post* discussed the matter.

"It is almost amusing to note the way in which Mayor Cauffiel of Johnstown seeks to reduce the disgust felt by liberal-minded people everywhere over his reported order to colored people of the city to leave the place unless they have lived there seven years," the *Post* said.

The growing outrage over the order spurred the attention of organizations like the American Civil Liberties Union and the National Association for the Advancement of Colored People. Both of those groups, along with others, wrote letters and lobbied to have Governor Gifford Pinchot and federal lawmakers investigate.

The NAACP was a relatively new organization, having begun in 1909. In establishing it, the activists challenged the color line and started a national struggle for full legal and civic equality. James Weldon Johnson took the NAACP's top position in 1920, and he was deeply involved in conversations regarding the future of black America and the search for effective activist methods. Johnson, the second black individual and first southerner to serve

James Weldon Johnson, executive secretary of the National Association for the Advancement of Colored People, was known for his colorful prose, poetry and advocacy. Johnson galvanized the organization to fight against persecution and discrimination throughout the country, including in Johnstown. *Library of Congress, Prints and Photographs Division, Washington, D.C.*

in an administrative position in the organization, brought fresh vision, vitality and a remarkable amount of experience to the NAACP. Dr. William G. Jordan said that Johnson was eloquent and militant.

"He was one of the great leaders of that time in the black community," Jordan said. "He wrote plays and novels. He was a leader of the Harlem Renaissance. I would say he was one of the more effective advocates during this time for his people."

Johnson had faced persecution. In 1902, he was nearly lynched for socializing with a white woman in Florida. As a traveling musician, he learned about the discrimination faced by African Americans across the nation.

His appointment as the executive secretary was a departure for the NAACP, which had been reluctant to appoint black people to the position. But there was a push to place an African American in the post, and Johnson was the most qualified of any member.[46]

When news of Johnstown reached the national NAACP, the organization acted swiftly to protect the lives, property and civil rights of the city's black residents. It rushed a special investigator there and wired Governor Pinchot and Mayor Cauffiel to tell them the order was an overuse of authority and pointed out that the only duty Cauffiel had was the apprehension and punishment of the guilty and that he had no authority in driving out black people, innocent or guilty, "whose only offense is that their skins are black."

The association's telegram demanded the mayor cease the hounding of African Americans:

> *Press dispatches in today's newspapers report that more than two thousand Negroes have left Johnstown as a result of your order that only Negroes resident in the city for seven years would be allowed to remain because of shooting of two policemen and wounding of four others, these crimes alleged to have been committed by Negroes.*
>
> *If the facts as reported above are correct, National Association for the Advancement of Colored People, with four hundred and fifty branches, and membership of one hundred thousand, composed of members of both races, vigorously protest against this high-handed injustice in such wholesale deportation. It appears to us that you have totally exceeded authority vested in you.*
>
> *It is the duty of the mayor and the other authorities of Johnstown to seek out and punish the guilty instead of punishing men whose only offense is that their skins are black. We respectfully urge that the hounding of colored citizens be stopped and the city of Johnstown cease making itself a tool for carrying out the threats of the Ku Klux Klan.*

In the postwar era, militancy took over parts of the African American community, including its activist segments. The NAACP had faith that equality and justice could be secured through the democracy. Sometimes people from within their ranks and outside of them criticized them for it. Some said that there had to be a fear that black men and women would fight back.

Other activists, including Marcus Garvey, who started the Universal Negro Improvement Association, mobilized the black community at sometimes a much faster pace than the NAACP because he appealed to their racial pride. James Weldon Johnson responded to Garvey's criticisms by emphasizing racial pride and unity. Garvey and the NAACP's leadership were often at odds. Garvey was the victim of bad press, according to Dr. Ralph Proctor. White newspapers—and even the *Pittsburgh Courier*—cast him as a person who wanted to force all black people back to Africa. In reality, Garvey spoke about the talented tenth going back, and he told them that they should do so voluntarily. Garvey was a victim of colorism—he was dark in a time when it wasn't popular to be extremely dark-skinned. The NAACP was mostly composed of light-skinned African Americans. The misperception shaped how his supporters were treated. There was violence toward them.

"In western Pennsylvania, Garveyites were treated the same as they were everywhere else," Dr. Proctor said. "They weren't popular and weren't treated well. They would make fun of them and harass them because they thought they wanted to send them back to Africa."

Garvey didn't think black people had a future in the American mainstream, which put him at fundamental odds with the NAACP, which had a central belief that African Americans could and should be included in the mainstream.

Garvey addressed the Johnstown matter at a speech in Liberty Hall in New York City on September 16. Garvey was a proponent of the "Back to Africa" movement. He argued that African Americans' quest for social equality in the United States was delusional and believed they must return to Africa to receive full emancipation. He used the Johnstown incident and other racially charged events in Tulsa, Oklahoma, and St. Louis, Missouri, as evidence to support his views.

Whites took hundreds of black lives in a race riot in St. Louis in 1917. They left countless more homeless. Two years before the Rosedale exodus, a terrible race riot took place in Tulsa, Oklahoma. It was the worst outbreak of racial violence in American history. White residents resented the economic success of black people and the prosperity in their neighborhoods. Marauding white people destroyed more than one thousand homes and businesses in the riot. The riots left nine thousand people homeless, according to the National Museum of African American History and Culture exhibit on the matter.

"If you don't want us in Johnstown, Pa., if you don't want us in Tulsa, if you don't want us in East St. Louis, we want ourselves where we want to be, and we are not going to remain here and create any trouble any longer than is necessary," Garvey said. "We are not going to leave now. All of us didn't come at the same time and therefore, all of us won't leave at the same time."

In Johnstown, Cauffiel remained obstinate.

Marcus Garvey was the leader of the United Negro Improvement Association, which championed the Back to Africa movement. This photo was taken in 1924. *George Grantham Bain Collection, Library of Congress Prints and Photographs Division, Washington, D.C.*

"I don't care what authority I have; for their own safety and the safety of the Johnstown public the Negroes are going out of this city," Cauffiel said. "They tell me I'm going to get into trouble. I don't care what they say. If the rest of them don't get out soon I'll arm police and send them into the colonies to walk the Negroes out of town at the point of gun."

THE GOVERNOR

W hen the NAACP's telegram reached Pennsylvania governor Gifford Pinchot on September 15, the tone revealed the outrage felt by the country's African Americans. The telegram mentioned the New York headlines and repeated what the organization told Cauffiel. During the whole ordeal, there was also a pressmen's strike at New York City newspapers. All the news that those publications had, which usually filled thirty-two pages, only filled eight. And those pages carried only the most important news of the world. Johnstown was consistently featured.

"The Association respectfully requests you to use all authority vested in your high office to correct this grievous injustice if the facts stated above are found to be true and to protect the Colored Citizens of Johnstown against the Ku Klux Klan's methods of Mayor Cauffiel," the telegram read.

Pinchot was primarily known as an environmentalist. He had been head of the Division of Forestry, and under President Theodore Roosevelt, he was named chief forester of the U.S. Forest Service. He was a close friend of Roosevelt, and he assumed that forests could produce timber while also being maintained for the future. In 1910, he became president of the National Conservation Association, a watchdog group over the development of public lands. Pinchot was elected governor of Pennsylvania in 1922. He received positive marks for his record on labor, public utility regulation and fiscal conservatism. He offended many by enforcing Prohibition. He also focused on providing relief to the unemployed.

Pennsylvania governor Gifford Pinchot in 1922. Pinchot was chiefly known as an environmentalist, but he was also a champion of progressive causes and a close friend of President Teddy Roosevelt. *Library of Congress, Prints and Photographs Division, Washington, D.C.*

Pinchot's ancestors fought against slavery, campaigned for Native American rights, provided free college education to some and supported civil rights organizations. His wife, the former Cornelia Bryce, was an ardent advocate of women's suffrage, birth control, civil rights and child labor reform. Cornelia Pinchot was a founding member of the Committee 100, which was dedicated to justice and equality for African Americans. She also helped increase the NAACP legal defense and education fund by $120,000 within the first seven years.

Pinchot didn't identify with the conservative old guard of the state during his gubernatorial campaign. But he also distanced himself from radicalism. He told his brother Amos, known for his extreme views, to make sure their perspectives were not seen as the same. No Pennsylvania governor ever began his administration with more public confidence. Liberals were drawn to him because of his association with the progressive cause. Conservatives liked him because of his focus on the economy and businesslike methods.

Pinchot worked sixteen hours a day seemingly with unlimited energy. He made himself available to the public with an open door policy. He set aside two hours on three days each week to talk to citizens about their problems. Pinchot's man-of-the-people approach was something he learned from Teddy Roosevelt. He emulated the former president and wanted his own policy to be known as a little "Square Deal" in honor of Roosevelt's famous campaign pledge.

The Pinchots were about as receptive to the NAACP as it would get.

But Cauffiel was a close friend of President Theodore Roosevelt, who elevated Pinchot on the national level as a leading forester. Roosevelt visited Cauffiel several times in Johnstown, according to the mayor's obituary, written by Eleanor Cauffiel Rutledge. Through his interactions with Roosevelt and in statewide politics, Cauffiel befriended Pinchot.

But in just about every way, Pinchot was the polar opposite of Cauffiel. Where Pinchot was cautious, Cauffiel was rash. Cauffiel was bigoted, while Pinchot and his wife pushed for equality. The mayor was polarizing, while the governor was widely popular. Though they were disparate in views and demeanor, they were the unlikeliest of friends. Politics makes strange bedfellows.

The situation was a delicate one. Pinchot had to condemn the act while navigating political waters. People from all over lobbied Pinchot to do something, with protests coming from as far away as Michigan. In Cauffiel's favor was the fact that Pinchot was vehemently opposed to the sale and use of alcohol. Pinchot almost fanatically believed in the wisdom of Prohibition. No governor of any state tried harder to keep the pledge. When he came into office in 1922, he made clear with his customary flair for the dramatic that law enforcement was a subject uppermost in his mind. He forced each person appointed to a state post to take an oath not to drink. Pinchot's heart was so deeply in enforcement that he had no sympathy for

Above: Pennsylvania governor Gifford Pinchot counted Johnstown mayor Joseph Cauffiel as a friend because of their mutual support for Prohibition. Pinchot received letters and telegrams from across the country from activists and civic leaders protesting the wholesale deportation of black and Mexican laborers from Johnstown. *Library of Congress, Prints and Photographs Division, Washington, D.C.*

Opposite: An early picture of Roger Baldwin, who founded the American Civil Liberties Union, in the *St. Louis Star and Times* on July 24, 1910. Baldwin and his organization registered a protest to the racial expulsion ordered by Johnstown mayor Joseph Cauffiel. *Newspapers.com.*

lukewarm enforcement of the Prohibition laws. So he appreciated some of Cauffiel's passion for the Eighteenth Amendment, though he disagreed with some of his more controversial tactics.

While he pondered all that, other activist organizations became involved in the matter. The board of the American Civil Liberties Union mentioned Johnstown when it gave a report for the week ending September 15. "Mayor Cauffiel of Johnstown, Pa., has made a name for himself by doing on a grand scale what petty officials are usually able to do unnoticed, namely excuse an illegal action against members of the community by the plea that he was forced to act quickly," the board said.[47]

The ACLU was born out of a fight to defend free speech during World War I, when protestors of the war effort were imprisoned or harassed by the government. It was officially established in 1920. The essential feature was a nonpartisan defense of the Bill of Rights. Roger Baldwin was its executive director. He was able to form the ACLU through his force of energy, charm and talent for organizing. His instincts set the course for the ACLU that continues today—a complex mixture of liberal social reform impulses with a conservative reverence for the Bill of Rights.[48]

The ACLU had been monitoring the exodus since it began and mentioned it in its report the week before when it said that fifteen black people were arrested in Johnstown for rioting. The ACLU board also discussed the mayor's order and said that two thousand people had left, which seemed to have become the agreed-upon figure by most parties at that point.

After *Johnstown Democrat* editor Warren Worth Bailey contacted the organization, it issued a protest to the mayor. The ACLU committee requested that the office take up the issue with various groups interested in helping African Americans and that further action would be taken only after conference with them.

"The organization, devoted to impartial administration of civil law and opposition to all race discrimination, wishes to know on what authority you order Negro residents less than seven years out of Johnstown and prohibit freedom of assemblage to Negroes," the telegram to the mayor read.

Prominent individuals throughout the country raised their voices, too. L. Hollingsworth Wood, a lawyer on Nassau Street in New York, sent a telegram to Governor Pinchot. Wood was a Quaker attorney and president of the National Urban League. His understanding of the situation was that it arose from a race riot, which remained a prevailing view among whites. Wood said he wanted to point out constructive methods of handling such situations. He said Cleveland and Pittsburgh were worried about similar circumstances. Wood also described the order as banishment. He said it drew attention in dramatic fashion to the real problem in government faced by all those in authority in the large industrial centers of the country. Wood spoke about how organized labor had not fought for the African Americans who came north because the union heads perceived them as strikebreakers.

"Of course in any body of men one must expect to find some percentage of criminal or semi-criminal individuals, and the Mayor of Johnstown, having discovered some, has adopted wholesale method of eliminating the colored part of his problem, but as you will readily see, one calculated to increase the problems of executives of other cities in Pennsylvania or the state government," Wood said.

The *Philadelphia Tribune* said the order violated the Constitution and was a blot on the fair name of Pennsylvania.

B.G. Collier, grand chancellor of the Grand Lodge Knights of Pythias in Pennsylvania, wrote the governor. The organization was a fraternal organization and secret society that began in Washington, D.C., in the 1800s. Collier said that Cauffiel's order prevented members of the Johnstown lodge from holding regular meetings and made it impossible for the officers to collect dues and endowment premiums. Collier criticized the Ku Klux Klan and Joseph Simmons, who said he was a friend of African Americans. Collier said blacks and whites voted for Pinchot because he believed in equal rights.

Collier told Pinchot he was directed to prepare whatever legal course was necessary to prevent enforcement of the order. Other telegrams of such nature came into the governor's office. Pinchot felt the pressure mounting. Upon receiving NAACP executive secretary James Weldon Johnson's telegram, Gifford Pinchot wired him back. He also contacted Cauffiel.

"Complaint has been lodged with me to protect that rights guaranteed by the Constitution of Pennsylvania have been set aside in Johnstown in connection with the expulsion of Mexicans and Negroes," Pinchot said to the mayor. "This is so serious a charge that I shall be obliged. If you will wire me to Milford a full account of exactly what took place together with the reasons for action taken."

The Reverend Robert B. St. Clair, president of the International Association for the Abolition of Racial Prejudice based in Detroit, sent a letter to Pinchot. St. Clair, a forty-nine-year-old pastor for the First Detroit Seventh Day Baptist

Church, was known for being active in Prohibition enforcement. Born in New York City, he entered the ministry in 1897 and was a pastor at the Detroit church since 1917. He was also an accomplished author.

"This is a most remarkable order," St. Clair said. "If we have to regard to our national naturalization laws, we note that it would be possible from our natives from the jungles of Africa or the wilds of certain of the South Sea Islands to enter this country and become full-fledged American citizens in five years' time.

"Yet by this ukase of your Johnstown mayor, it requires two years longer for colored citizens of this country, and native born at that, to effect municipal naturalization in the city of which he is the chief magistrate than it does for foreigners to become federally naturalized. This, to us, is inexplicable."

St. Clair said that he was a white man with ancestry dating back to the colonial days. He was the son of one Civil War veteran on the Union's side and the nephew of four other veterans, two of whom were native Pennsylvanians and who worked in Pennsylvania regiments. St. Clair aided in the religious work after the great Johnstown Flood in 1889.

Joseph G. Graves, president of the Graves Indian Herb Medicine Company in Philadelphia, said the whole country was shocked at what happened, and he called Cauffiel a disgrace to Pennsylvania. He singled out the mayor's recent quotes in a Philadelphia newspaper, the *North American*. Graves said that during the First World War, when German spies committed arson, not one German was ordered out of the country, state or community.

"Governor, you have been silent on this matter," Graves told the governor. "I know not what your reason is for not finding a solution. I appeal to you because you are the chief executive of the State by the people and for the people regardless of race, color or creed. I trust whatever action you may see fit to take you will see that those unfortunate people will be given a square deal."

Dr. Andrew Sandoval-Strausz, Latino studies professor at Penn State, said that while there were federal laws in place to protect the rights of minorities at the time, they were often ignored by local leaders. Even if the end goal was racist, any action toward that end was justifiable.

"Many local sheriffs and townspeople just want to collectively use vigilante means. There is really no one to stop them," he said. "And the federal government doesn't enforce civil rights in this period. They're pretty much hands off. So in a rural city in Pennsylvania, the citizenry and leaders are the law. This was motivated by racial hatred. It's unlawful. But they can get away with it."

Nellie Gazzam, chairwoman of the Independent Republican Women of the eighth ward of Philadelphia, sent a letter to the governor. Gazzam described the situation as superfluous.

In Philadelphia, at the George C. Cornish American Legion Post 292, the members assembled in regular meeting and voted unanimously to declare Cauffiel's action illegal, and its leaders compared it to the expulsion of the French from Acadia by the British. The members said Cauffiel acted arbitrarily and in an unconstitutional manner. They told Pinchot that he should take immediate steps to ensure his citizens' rights.

Señor Don Manuel G. Tellez, Mexican chargé d'affaires, sent a note to the American embassy on September 15. Tellez objected to the coupling of Mexicans with blacks in the expulsion order.

"Mexicans are not negroid in race or in sympathies," he declared. "The percentage of Negroes is far lower in Mexico than in the United States, and there is no justification for Mayor Cauffiel's act in classifying them with Negroes, other than the fact that they have been working in the same steel plant. They do not live with Negroes, but by themselves."

Several of the expelled Mexicans appealed directly to their embassy to secure permission for them to return to Johnstown and to guarantee protection for them after. Others who refused to leave asked for protection, too. Tellez instructed the Mexican consul in Philadelphia to look into the situation. The Mexican embassy staff told the consul in Philadelphia to proceed to Johnstown and report on the situation. F.A. Pesqueira, representing the consul, also telegrammed Governor Pinchot.

"I have wired the mayor of Johnstown asking protection for my nationals in expulsion from said city," Pesqueira said. "Respectfully request your assistance in investigation of causes that have brought about expulsion and also your orders to state authorities for protecting citizens of Mexico."

The Mexican government protest was not the only criticism Pinchot had to contend with. People and organizations nationwide denounced the Johnstown banishment. It was a wave of anger that eventually forced Pinchot to confront his friend, the mayor.

Cauffiel said he merely advised Mexicans to leave because he felt it was hard to distinguish them from African Americans and he was afraid they would suffer in any uprising against the black community. In police court one morning during his ban's enforcement, the mayor ordered a Mexican brought before him on a minor charge to leave the state within five hours.

William Phillips, the acting U.S. secretary of state, sent Pinchot a telegram from Washington, D.C., that told him about the Mexican government's reaction to the order. "Mexican embassy here complains that mayor of Johnstown has ordered all Mexicans and Negroes who have not resided at least seven years in said place to leave. And that in consequence many Mexicans have already left," Phillips said. "Others are preparing to do so, while still others are in jail. Embassy states that requests of Mexican consul in Philadelphia to extend protection to Mexican citizens condemned."

The Mexican embassy wanted the order to be withdrawn.

"I do not doubt that you will make prompt investigation and take suitable steps under the laws of your state to correct any injustice which may have been done to these Mexican citizens," Phillips told Pinchot, "and to afford them adequate protection in their rights."

Few of the Mexicans in Johnstown actually left the city. The heads at Bethlehem Steel took steps to prevent them from becoming involved in trouble. Cauffiel was satisfied that some were buying homes, and he did not want to treat them unjustly. The mayor's critics said the Mexicans simply paid no attention to him.

Pinchot announced shortly after receiving the telegram that Mexicans expelled from Johnstown would be permitted to return and those who did not leave would not be bothered. He reassured the Mexican embassy through the Mexican consul at Philadelphia. Tellez expressed his gratification at the prompt action of the State Department and the governor. Unless unexpected developments arose, he considered the incident closed, he told reporters.

The Johnstown affair made the front pages of many Mexican newspapers, including *El Informador* in Jalisco. They reported that, according to information provided to the American government by the mayor and the governor, it was all a question of simple alarm and a bad interpretation. The reports told them that the Mexicans in the city had not been the victims of any attacks, nor had they been exposed to danger in any way. The U.S. State Department wanted to make sure Cauffiel didn't hurt relationships and negotiations with Mexico.

Pinchot received criticism from some quarters in the black community who felt he had only acted when a foreign government became involved. It was as if he was more concerned with what the leaders of Mexico thought of Pennsylvania than what happened to black citizens. The *Chicago Defender* published a critical editorial called "When a Protest Counts":

> *In justice to the governor, we might be willing to believe that he intended to act with a sense of justice before receiving the Mexican note of protest. Yet, on the other hand, we are impelled to recognize the fact that his action*

did not come prior to the note. It seems that the protests from such powerful organizations as the National Association for the Advancement of Colored People elicited no response nor did the appeals of thousands of individuals.

The editorial said that Pinchot took Mexico's telegrams more seriously because that country was a market for American goods. The *Defender* claimed Pinchot acted because he wanted to respond to business leaders who thought an attack on Mexicans in the United States would hurt trade with Mexico.

Cauffiel did not answer the telegrams from the Mexican embassy. He bunkered down to withstand all the flak he caught from the press, especially from big cities.

"What does New York, Philadelphia and Pittsburgh know about the situation in Johnstown?" the mayor said. "I'm the one that is responsible for law and order, and I'm going to see that it's preserved here."

Despite the mayor's complaints, condemnation only grew. Everyone was paying attention to the little city east of Pittsburgh. The *St. Louis Post-Dispatch* said the country was watching what was happening in Johnstown. They said it was a dangerous experiment that aroused a worse feeling between the races than otherwise existed. They predicted it would make its way into the courts, which would hold the action unconstitutional. The *Hamilton Evening Journal* in Ohio said that Mayor Cauffiel had ditched the Constitution. The *Journal* said trouble arose because of the importation of laborers and the sense of competition between new and old workers in industrial communities.

The Equal Rights League, a black organization in Boston, sent telegrams to Pinchot and President Calvin Coolidge asking them to take action. The message to Pinchot read that "any sort of punishment from the chief executive of a city visited on persons not charged with any crime or misdemeanor is a violation of the charter, despotic and illegal under the state constitution."

They asked Pinchot to take over the administration by martial law. President Coolidge was asked to "exert the prestige and power of his position to protect citizens of the United States from being deprived of life, liberty and property without the process of law in violation of the Fourteenth Amendment."

Though the president wouldn't go on record about what his thoughts were on the matter, Pinchot became the chief political figure acting against the Johnstown mayor. The hopes of Cauffiel's critics rested with him.

REPUDIATION

The day before the primary was held on September 18, the *Johnstown Tribune* published an editorial discussing what voters should consider going into the polling places. "It is a solemn obligation which is presented to the voters, and one that every good citizen should undertake with the good of the city and county at heart. Mistakes made tomorrow are very apt to be perpetuated in the November election."

All of the candidates for mayor were well-known men. The editorial charged some of the candidates with corruption and indirectly addressed the order given by Mayor Cauffiel. "Efforts have been made to confuse, to delude the average voter by introduction of falsely raised 'issues,'" the editors wrote.[49]

During the lead-up to the election, Cauffiel's opponents accused him of grandstanding. The election was one of the hottest and closest fought in the county's history. It was ten or twelve hours after the polls closed before officials received sufficient returns to enable even the closest observer to pick the winners. But voters did overwhelmingly reject Cauffiel.[50]

In the race for mayor, the other candidates received double or triple what he garnered. He trailed fourth in the race. The *Tribune* wrote about what most citizens thought in the aftermath of the election:

> *Governor Pinchot took a hand in the affair a few days ago, and demanded an explanation. The Mexican Government has made representations to the United States Government over the affair, demanding protection for its citizens and guardance of their rights. So, Mayor Cauffiel has become*

an international character. Comments in every paper which has come to hand on the "get out" order are a unit in condemning the Mayor and in disparaging the city.

It is a question whether this sort of publicity is good for the town which has as its slogan "The Friendly City."[51]

When news about Cauffiel's defeat reached the offices of the *Pittsburgh Courier*, the staff praised the people of Johnstown. Vann and his staff later penned an editorial titled "Johnstown Repudiates Mayor":

He was running on his record, and his declarations to the people included some of his radical views. The voters defeated him decisively, and he awakes to find that he is not any longer a mayor of any town, and the Negroes and Mexicans whom he ordered out of the city are living quietly in Johnstown, free from the attacks of a demented mayor. These sudden uprisings are to be expected from time to time.

They represent the lack of Americanism in our great country, and their appearances here and there but serve notice upon the people that we have not yet digested all the elements within our borders. The mayor of Johnstown is no more. The people have disposed of him, and the little town of flood fame is operating under a normal pulse once more.

Though they gave credit to the Johnstown electorate, the *Courier*'s coverage short-changed or failed to mention the fact that close to two thousand African Americans left. It was unknown who else was complicit. When one looks at the facts, the order had to have received support from a sizable portion of the public or from law enforcement to be as effective as it was. So it seemed like the person who was solely blamed—Cauffiel—drew attention away from some of the other parties who enabled him. One could argue that it wasn't the order itself that caused his defeat. It was the negative attention from newspapers across the country that did him in.

The *Courier* described Cauffiel in other coverage as a crawfish that retreated to its lair under the scourging lash of rigid investigation and public protest. They called him a despot.

"His tyrannical edict to Negroes and Mexicans to 'leave Johnstown if they were residents of less than seven years' failed to gain him the crown of glory and badge of honor he expected, for his world of dreams has come tumbling down upon him and he has scrambled out of the debris weakened, beatened, his Nemesis, DEFEAT, ready to take him by the hand," the *Courier* declared.

The *Courier* praised the governor, the Mexican government, the Washington embassy and the NAACP, declaring defeat was miserable and a poison thorn in Cauffiel's side. "Today Johnstown is quiet—the excitement of the last two weeks has subsided, and the deserted homes of thousands of colored people are the only evidences that the peace and quiet of the community had been disturbed."

"The mayor's 'high-handed and arbitrary action' has been properly handled," the reporter continued. "Public opinion in the North regards the result as far-reaching as concerns the interests of the Negro laborer in the North; and nips in the bud the propaganda of the South that the Negro migrant is receiving ill treatment at the hands of Northern labor."

Though Cauffiel was beaten handily in the primaries, he remained the mayor of the city until the beginning of the next year. As such, he still had the power to enforce his order, which made many, including Governor Pinchot, realize that they had to act to protect the rights of the minorities who still lived in Johnstown. Pinchot sent a telegram to Cauffiel on September 19 asking for the facts of the order and the details of its execution. Pinchot asked state police for information.

Meanwhile, officials at the national NAACP headquarters wired the Pittsburgh branch about the matter. In the telegram, they urged other leaders to use Cauffiel's defeat as recruitment material: "National office urges Pittsburgh branch to capitalize on this great victory in so dramatic a fight. Achievement should gain many members for your branch. If you arrange big meeting, one of national officers will come and speak if you wish and we urge you act immediately. Advise us of what your branch will do."

The *Branch Bulletin*, a publication of the NAACP, said the organization brought Cauffiel down: "What happened at Johnstown ought to stir determination in every branch and individual member of the NAACP and particularly in those who are not members."

The article said more black people would have been driven from their homes and jobs had they not acted. The accomplishment served as a deterrent for other chief executives who could act so rashly, the bulletin writer said:

> *Successful there other cities would undoubtedly have followed Mayor Cauffiel's despicable example. Again, had not the NAACP by years of unremitting toil established a reputation as being the great and powerful organization that it is, Gov. Pinchot would hardly have acted so promptly. It is no discredit to him that he knew the NAACP's contention was right*

and was backed up by numbers and power. The press stated that so many organizations and individuals wired him but so far as is known he replied as he did only to the NAACP. All these are but additional reasons for strong, active, alert branches for it must be remembered that "eternal vigilance is the price of liberty."

The Reverend R.R. Wright Jr., editor of the *Christian Recorder* in Philadelphia, sent a letter to the governor on September 20:

I have read by the papers your stand in regards to the absurd order of the Mayor of Johnstown, Penna., to expel Negroes who have come to that city during the past seven years. Both personally and as a representative of the African Methodist Episcopal Church, the oldest and largest organization of Negroes of this country, I wish to heartily commend your stand. I shall take occasion to express this commendation in the columns of our official organ THE CHRISTIAN RECORDER *in our next issue. Those of us who belong to the Negro race and who see our brethren coming from the South, fleeing from the lyncher and the Ku Klux, are glad that we live in a state whose governor upholds the constitution of the United States, and is not afraid to speak for justice for those who are unjustly oppressed.*

We assure you that we are doing everything in our power to help to properly adjust the newcomers to their new situations and if there is anything which you, yourself, have in mind, we stand ready to give our cooperation.

Cassius Ward, pastor of the Ebenezer Baptist Church in Boston, also sent a letter to Pinchot: "The country has been horrified and a group of the most loyal citizens in America humiliated at the drastic action of the Mayor of Johnstown, Pennsylvania, who ordered all Negroes who had not been resident for seven years to leave the city," Ward wrote. "We request you to investigate this matter and to make it possible for those innocent people to return to their homes. Such action on the part of the mayor was an abridgment of their constitutional rights and should not be permitted by the great state of Pennsylvania."

Cauffiel continued to come under fire from journalists. The *Muncie Evening Press* wrote about him in an editorial called "What Would an Alien Think?"

The thrust of the piece was what a foreigner would think of the country's treatment of labor and its citizens if his or her first impressions were from the situation in Johnstown. The editorial board at the *Evening Press* said law-breaking was more likely now among immigrants who saw that public officials were not bound by the law. They said that guilty men and women should be held accountable but that should not be given priority over defending innocent people.

"Punishment for the guilty should be swift—and in this instance it appears to have been very swift and effective—but it should not be swifter than the giving of protection to the innocent."

The forces of intolerance in Johnstown continued to demonstrate, even though the majority of people had expressed that they did not sympathize with their position. The Ku Klux Klan burned another cross near Rosedale as the national furor grew around Cauffiel. The Klan was firmly behind Cauffiel's decision to order and force black people to leave. But Cauffiel's treatment of blacks was not going over well with some parts of the community. One reader sent a letter to the *Johnstown Democrat* deploring it: "To make Johnstown a real friendly city, religious, color and race prejudice should be abolished. There is too much prejudice along those lines. Housing conditions and good streets, without friendly feeling toward your neighbor regardless of religion, color or race, mean nothing."

After the governor wired him, Cauffiel wrote back explaining his order and its background:

> *Johnstown has been over run by many Negroes from the South, paroled from the southern prisons. Inside of three weeks time three of our officers have been buried, two are lying in the hospitals, mortally wounded. One is recovering. All this is due to a shooting affair by a Negro crazed by moonshine and dope.*
>
> *Our citizens were aroused and we had difficulty in maintaining order. The citizens could not distinguish between Mexicans and the copper colored Negroes and for their own protection and the preservation of the good name of our city they were advised to leave. Only the lawless ones were advised to leave.*
>
> *I have endeavored to combat against this the best I know how. We appealed to your State Police and had six of your men for about a week. The captain of our police department is lying at the point of death from a bullet wound inflicted by the Negro now dead and the minds of people are still stirred to the utmost.*[52]

Cauffiel said he couldn't predict what would happen to the local black community if Fink died and alleged more responsibility for the situation rested with the governor.

If your State Police Department would try to close up the booze joints and dope joints now existing in Franklin Borough, adjacent to Johnstown, and one of the worst hell holes in the State, we would not have had this trouble. You can readily see why I have restricted the colored people from having any meetings of any kind except church services. I do not know what the press has stated to you but I have given you my text in full.

My duty is to preserve peace and order and you can readily see how difficult the proposition is with characters of this kind and nature. Our native Negroes and some of the others are law-abiding and there is no complaint against them. It is only the lawless pack that have no regard for law and order or life and there was no discrimination against the black race. After this trouble it was a difficult proposition to hold the citizens in obeyance.

Asked by reporters following the election if he would modify his stand, the mayor said, "No, I have nothing to apologize for; I will make no excuse to anyone. I did what I saw was my duty and I will continue to order every Negro who has not lived here seven years to get out and stay out."

The *Pittsburgh Courier* remained critical.

"Joseph Cauffiel, self-styled 'Ivan the Terrible,' arch persecutor, has been called to account for his infamous edict ordering the wholesale deportation of Negroes from this city," one article began.

It continued, "The despicable mayor was further rebuked yesterday in the election in which he was swamped for a second term. Not only Negroes, but also the whites registered their harsh disapproval of this iniquitous modern Biblical Haman, who has attempted to inject poisonous venom into the hearts of the local citizenry against a peaceful people who come at their own invitation. It is believed in authentic circles that the mayor issued his ignominious decree bidding for the vote of the Ku Klux Klan and its sympathizers. The returns of yesterday's voting showed that he had made himself very unpopular and was trailing in fourth or fifth place."

The *Morning Register* in Eugene, Oregon, printed an editorial about the whole ordeal on September 29. It said that those who were ordered out obeyed without question, fleeing with much inconvenience and loss. The rest were in a state of terror.

"The mayor's provocation seems to have been great. The influx of Negroes, many of them undesirables, has led to serious problems of housing, health, morals and crime. It is natural to want to get rid of troublemakers of any race. But is the remedy any better than the disease? The mayor's action is plainly illegal, declared so by the governor of the state."

The events in Johnstown riveted the American public. Everyone seemed to have an opinion. Most of it was against Cauffiel. But despite the negative publicity about the Johnstown incident indicating that racism seemed to ebb during the early 1920s, it and other events, including the race riots in St. Louis and Tulsa, Oklahoma, were a testament that bigotry endured.

And between 1890 and 1940, one person was lynched every four days in America. The country had a long way to go before it exited the darkest period of racial inequality in a post-slavery era.

GROWING OUTRAGE

Other civil liberties organizations condemned the mayor. The Labor Defense and Free Speech Council of Western Pennsylvania called the act outrageous.

"The sinews, blood and tears of the Negro workers helped to make this country what it is," it said in a letter published in the *Pittsburgh American*. "For two hundred and fifty years, the Negro toiled in the U.S., helping to clear the forests, build the roads, raise the cotton and lay the railroad tracks. The Negro is entitled to the rights as guaranteed to the people of this country by the constitution of the U.S."

White workers historically dominated labor unions largely because African Americans were viewed as people who hurt collective bargaining efforts. The Labor Defense and Free Speech Council of Western Pennsylvania was unique.

"It's fair to say unions representing skilled laborers were not representing black workers," said Dr. Spencer Crew. "I think it's fair to say that African-Americans didn't get great representation from the unions. There was some antipathy between the groups. Sometimes they were brought in as strikebreakers."

Meanwhile, in Johnstown, Cauffiel took heat from quarters inside the city, outside the city, in the state, out of the state, in the country and outside of it.

"The Emperor of Johnstown, whether a Kleagle of a Ku Klux Klan or not, has no authority by which he may drive or warn law-abiding Negroes and Mexicans from the precincts of that city," the *Philadelphia Evening Bulletin* wrote in an editorial. "The fact that the objects of his warning are taking his advice and leaving without any trouble, or that public sentiment in Johnstown tacitly gives assent to the program, does not alter that truth."

The *Bulletin* said he had no authority to do it, regardless of whether there was a race riot. It said one aspect of the Johnstown situation had been overlooked. The black people and Mexicans had come at the request of a great industrial enterprise. Bethlehem and other industries had been forced to seek labor because of expansion and to some extent the abolition of the twelve-hour day at the plant. The Johnstown steel industry faced a short labor market, made abnormally short by the enforcement of the quota immigration law against the inflow of unskilled labor from Europe. Black and Mexican workers were the only labor pool they could draw from.

The *Daily Times* in Davenport, Iowa, said that Johnstown had been greatly stirred up, and for a time, mob violence and race rioting were feared. It concluded that Cauffiel's solution to the problem was that fewer black people meant less danger of trouble. The paper said it would be hard to enforce the order unless he had support of the Klan, which would only intensify racial feeling, and discussed the influx of black labor from the South, and the crime wave that came with it. The *Press and Sun-Bulletin* in Binghamton, New York, took the mayor to task for different reasons than most newspapers. While most condemned the banishment as a civil rights injustice, the newspaper said the mayor was passing along the troublemakers in his community to others. It described the Mexicans and black people in Johnstown as "refuse."

Dr. Spencer Crew said the negative portrayal of African Americans as subhuman was a result of other factors affecting whites living in those communities.

"What you're seeing is a smokescreen for other issues," he said. "One it was competition for jobs. And there was also competition for housing. So when that happens, people find other things to use to express the frustrations over competition. So you look for negative descriptors for why it's okay to run them out of town. And really it's the competition for those other things that are the base for what's in play."

The *Star Tribune* in Minneapolis said Cauffiel's order mocked the Constitution. The *News Journal* in Delaware compared Cauffiel to Benito Mussolini and General Primo Riviera, of Spain—two oppressive fascists in Europe. The paper mused that Johnstown had the flavor of dictatorship. It praised Cauffiel's political rivals in Johnstown, William H. Sunshine and Louis Franke, who were both more liberal.

Despite the widespread condemnation, hidden from the newspapers' castigations was the fact that many of the states these publications were in also had a history of racial cleansings and expulsions. In his definitive account of the subject, *Sundown Towns: A Hidden Dimension of American Racism*, James Loewen chronicles the phenomenon from 1890 until 1940, which he characterized as the low point for American race relations. States like Illinois, Indiana and even California and Washington had incidents in which races or religious groups were expelled wholesale from communities. Though the incident in Johnstown had drawn national attention and seemed weird to most, it was not uncommon during that era.

People continued to send letters to Cauffiel. Walter Borton of Philadelphia penned one. He told the mayor that he wasn't being a "destructive critic, but one who would like to help you in your very difficult problem."

Borton said Cauffiel's order was unjust.

Pinchot received telegrams from religious leaders in Illinois, who, after meeting at an annual conference in Danville, praised the governor. Chas S. MacFarland, Worth M. Tippy and George E. Haynes of the Social Service Commission and the Race Relations Commission sent Pinchot a joint telegram on September 20.

"We congratulate you heartily upon your determination as reported to the press to protect constitutional rights of Negro citizens in Johnstown," they telegrammed. "We are convinced that the church forces of the country of all denominations will endorse and earnestly support you in taking such steps as may be necessary in carrying out this policy if facts be as reported the expulsion of Negroes from Johnstown would constitute a dangerous precedent for every state and community in our country. Firm action now may prevent future trouble."

Cauffiel defied the national press and activist organizations.

"I don't care what authority I have; for their own safety and for the safety of the Johnstown public the Negroes are going out of this city. Most of them are out now and the rest are going fast," Cauffiel declared when he was asked to answer protests of the NAACP and other organizations protecting constitutional privileges.

The mayor pulled out a desk drawer and showed a reporter a scattered array of telegrams.

"See these," he said. "They are protests from all over the country, calling me a second 'czar of Russia,' a 'Kaiser,' and every other thing."

"They tell me I'm going to get in trouble," Cauffiel continued. "I don't care what they say. I wish some of them were here to get into the holes of vice that had been set up right in this city and near it by hordes of imported Negroes. Their colonies are lined with dives for the sale of moonshine and dope. That has to stop and the Negroes responsible for it must leave the city. If the rest of them don't get out soon, I'll arm police and send them into the colonies to walk the Negroes out of town at the point of gun."

Cauffiel said that the police wouldn't be able to stop the inevitable crime wave during the winter if black people remained. He said that the Cambria plant in Johnstown was running slack and that men were being laid off. Thousands of the migrants coming in weren't needed and wouldn't be for some time to come, according to Cauffiel.

"What are thousands of idle Negroes and Mexicans, stimulated by poison liquor and dope, going to do in Johnstown this winter? Given the chance they are going to steal, ravish and terrorize. I'm not the only one who isn't going to give them the chance."

Cauffiel blasted the steel companies and the agents who brought the black workers. "Imported labor is a failure," he said. "Bethlehem knows it now, and I've known it for some time. As mayor of this city, I am not going to stand idle and allow the South to dump its criminals and riff-raff into Johnstown. The Negroes can stay where they belong. That's in the South. The old time Negroes in this city never gave us any trouble, but the scum that has been brought here is not going to remain while I am mayor. And I want all Negroes not here yet to know that there's no use in coming."[53]

Empty shacks in Johnstown's black settlements, a continual exodus of newly arrived black residents and the absence of African American visitors to families living within the city limits of Johnstown bore evidence that Cauffiel's order had been sadly effective.

Cauffiel faced more scrutiny with each passing day. Dean Kelly Miller, the professor who had visited Johnstown to observe living conditions there, said the fact that Cauffiel ignored the housing arrangements for so long made the Rosedale shooting inevitable.

"I was prepared at any moment to hear of some dreadful happening in Johnstown," Miller said. "The fault of the situation and the responsibility therefore rests upon the controlling citizens of the community who allow their fellow man to live on such a depraved level of existence. The outbreak of any mode of crime, though appalling, is but the logical outcome of a degraded environment."

"The vindictive mayor of Johnstown is breathing out vengeance upon the whole racial contingent because of the criminal outbreak of a few. He would better serve his city, state and nation by remedying the environment which breeds the criminal rather than himself becoming the greater criminal by violating every law of God or man."

Cauffiel admitted that there was a discriminatory aspect to his order.

"While I realize this order may not be fair to all," he said, "I feel it is for the safety of all that every Negro that has not lived here for seven years pack up his belongings and get out at once. We cannot tell and we have no way of telling how many of those Negroes shipped in have criminal records until we get them in some scrap or other."

Associated Press reporter P.M. Young of Pittsburgh spent a day in Johnstown. The mayor told him the order was just a request. Young interviewed Chief Briney and many others to get to the bottom of the situation. The chief was noncommittal about whether he approved, although he gave the impression that he was not in entire accord with the mayor. Young visited Rosedale and talked with black residents. He saw that a considerable number of houses were vacant and was told that many people had left.

Young failed to obtain from Cauffiel a copy of his communication to the governor. The mayor said Pinchot should give it to the press instead of him. Cauffiel denied that there was a political motivation behind his decisions. Cauffiel tried to emphasize that it wasn't a blanket racist order. The residency figure of seven years or more showed that it was just the black newcomers from the South.

"My action was not directed against the Negroes who had made their homes here before exodus from the South began seven years ago," Cauffiel said. "That is why I put the residence figure at seven years. These people were alright but the influx from the South brought bad people. Among them were dopesters, moonshiners and other kinds of lawbreakers. We were unable to weed out all the band and I decided to send them back home. I know that among them were men paroled from prison. The fellow who killed our policemen was a paroled convict."

Even if he was just targeting southern migrants, Cauffiel was seemingly oblivious to the fact that most of Johnstown's population wouldn't know the length of residency for a black person on sight. His words inflamed their worst hatreds, with many showing hostility to the black community regardless of how long they lived there.

It seemed like western Pennsylvania would be a much better place for migrants who came. But they found in Johnstown, and elsewhere, that racial discrimination was widespread. Judges throughout the area often used indecent language and disparaged them much like Cauffiel. Johnstown had grown racially polarized over the previous seven years. And the order was the culmination of that.

SOUTHERN PROPAGANDA

Southerners took the banishment as a chance to create propaganda. They had lost a great deal of cheap labor during the Great Migration, and any event that showcased racism up north was used as material for why black southerners should stay. J.S. Wannamaker, president of the American Cotton Association, wrote a letter to Gifford Pinchot registering his protest two days after the governor ordered an investigation.

"The action taken at Johnstown is not only illegal and unjust, but followed to its logical conclusion is subversive of all constitutional rights guaranteed to American citizens. That the victims of it are persons of the negro race renders it in a manner a matter in which the Southern people are peculiarly concerned: for it is in the South that a vast majority of the negro population resides, and it is to the people of this section that the Afro-American must ultimately look for sympathy, protection and aid in the solution of the problems that are peculiarly his own," Wannamaker wrote.[54]

Wannamaker viewed southern history without accounting for the lynch mobs that brutally took thousands of black lives and the group of hooded men that terrorized minority communities.

Roughly 450,000 to 500,000 black southerners relocated to the North between 1915 and 1918. More than 700,000 more came during the 1920s. The migration created a great deal of resentment among southern white farmers and plantation owners. Newspapers there said black people had a better chance at advancement in the South. They carried cartoons vilifying northerners for their treatment of black people. Black newspapers up north

An informal picture of J.S. Wannamaker, president of the American Cotton Association. He was also a member of the National Council of the National Economic League. Wannamaker registered his protest to Governor Gifford Pinchot about the Johnstown racial expulsion as an effort to improve the perception of the South insofar as its treatment of African Americans was concerned. *Library of Congress, Prints and Photographs Division, Washington, D.C.*

responded in kind. The *Chicago Defender* printed a dispatch from Selma, Alabama, saying, "The White people of the extreme South are becoming alarmed over the steady moving of race families out of the mineral belt. Hundreds of families have left during the past few months and the stream is continuing. Every effort is being made to have them stay, but the discrimination and the race prejudice continues as strong as ever."[55]

In previous letters to newspapers, Wannamaker alternated between calling slavery "galling" and continuing to state that the southern economy was much more stable during that time. He presented himself frequently as both a champion of the black tenant farmer as well as the cotton plantation owner.

"The South has not forgotten, and can never forget the debt of gratitude which it owes the Negro race," Wannamaker continued. "As slaves it served faithfully for generations. In the hour of the South's greatest stress—while the War between the States was in progress—the Negroes gave an example of faithful service and devotion not duplicated by the conduct of any other subject race in similar circumstances in the history of the world."

Dr. Spencer Crew said the South created a negative perception of the treatment black workers received in the North. The cotton kings clung to the power that they slowly lost to northern industrial leaders.

"In the South, they weren't happy about losing this free labor," Crew said. "They tried to point that it wasn't a good place to go. Living conditions were terrible. It was cold. They needed to stay in the South because it was in their own economic benefit. For white farmers, African-Americans were important for their success."

Wannamaker argued that the South was more tolerant.

"The Negro is not held responsible in the South for the outrages in which he was tutored and led by the carpet-bag regime," Wannamaker wrote. "The impression entertained by some people that the relations between the Negroes and the whites of the South are unfriendly is wholly erroneous."

Wannamaker discussed how the impoverishment of the South was the fault of northerners who came during Reconstruction. Any bad things black people did during that time were the fault of those carpetbaggers, according to Wannamaker. He said that northern hypocrisy was on display in Johnstown. He said black people went north because of economic necessity instead of white hostility.

He urged Pinchot to push for state and federal prosecution. He offered to pay for the legal expenses of black defendants in Johnstown. Wannamaker later sent a telegram to the governor to tell him that he and the Cotton Association would pay any fines impressed upon black people in Johnstown as well as transportation costs to travel back to the sections of the South where they were needed. He asked Pinchot to release the information to the press.

Cauffiel sentenced twenty black men to serve in chain gangs. It brought a direct response from Wannamaker, who said southern leaders would pay for legal counsel for black people who were criminally accused in Johnstown.

Mark Hersey, an associate professor at Mississippi State University who specializes in agricultural and African American history, said the southern leaders at the time were hypocritical and asserted it was better for African Americans in the North. Hersey noted there was a huge fear of the Great Migration among Southern farmers.

"The desire to keep African-Americans in the South stems from a desire for labor," Hersey said. "There is a fear of what will happen without it.

The second part is identity. There is a lost cause mythology. They're proud of being Southern. The Civil War was a noble cause. There wasn't a bad side. So these men are thinking of themselves as cotton men. And that was associated with black labor. These people also generally believed that it was beneficial for African-Americans to stay in the South."

Southern politicians addressed what happened in Johnstown. Malcolm R. Patterson, one-time governor of Tennessee, included the action of a Milwaukee judge who told black defendants they were not wanted in the city in his criticism:

> *I do not know of anything that has ever occurred in the South that for cold-blooded brutality equals the deliverances of the Johnstown mayor and the Milwaukee judge. An act of vengeance in the South is bad enough but this passes with the death of the victim of its wrath, and never extends to the race, but we are treated by these Northern spectators to race prejudice which embrace all who come within its full influences, and too this proceeds from officials clothed with power and responsibility.*

He added that Cauffiel didn't respect the law and was incapable of exercising restraint:

> *Answering the Johnstown mayor we are not sending Negroes to the North. This statement is a falsehood pure and simple. We regret here in the South to see them go on our own account and for their sakes. The Negroes have been lured away by Northern mills and factories, whose only interest in them was their labor and what advantage could be gained thereby. This is the only use for the Negro and when this fails, the Negro is left to the mercy of the tides. These are bad now and they will get worse as the Negro will find his sorrow. There is but one place for the Negro as a race and that is in the South, the land of his birth.*

T.D. Peets, the secretary of the Hazlehurst Chamber of Commerce in Mississippi, also sent a telegram to Pinchot condemning the action. Peets said only guilty people should be made to suffer from a crime. He said his organization would help provide legal counsel for black people accused of crimes in Johnstown during the order's enforcement.

Other southerners followed Wannamaker's lead. The *Winston County Signal* in Mississippi said that the expulsion was a sample of what southern black people received at the hands of northern people. They began a column with

Cauffiel's quotes. The *Montgomery Advertiser* took Cauffiel to task as well in an editorial titled "Mistreating our Southern Negroes."

The *Houston Post* said that thousands of black people traveled southward because of the hostile attitude of northern towns, and the paper speculated that the migration had ended. The *Post* said that incidents like the one in Johnstown gave southern newspapers propaganda material. The editors refrained from printing stories about it because they thought black people had a right to seek better conditions of living. But they doubted there was a warm welcome in the North except in cases where cheap labor was in demand. They pointed out that labor unions were never friendly to black people.

The *Courier-Journal* in Louisville, Kentucky, published an editorial titled "Negroes at the North."

The newspaper said Johnstown was as famous nationally as it had been during the great flood of 1889. It then alluded to Booker T. Washington, who was one of the most important thinkers in the late nineteenth century. He founded the Tuskegee Institute, a black school in Alabama that trained teachers. He was an advisor to Presidents Theodore Roosevelt and William Howard Taft. While other black leaders like W.E.B. DuBois emphasized reforming the system to combat institutional racism, Washington emphasized self-reliance among African Americans. Some black intellectuals criticized him for not acknowledging that the system was rigged in many ways against the black community. The *Courier-Journal* stated that Washington thought the South was the best region in the country for black people, and the editorial claimed Washington thought white people in the South were their best friends.

The *News Leader* in Staunton, Virginia, said that if any mayor in the South had brutally ordered two thousand of its black citizens out, he would have been ridiculed in northern newspapers. The newspaper inaccurately stated that northern and western newspapers hadn't been harsh enough in their criticism of Cauffiel, claiming that only one or two newspapers there condemned him. The newspaper pointed out the lack of legal action against Cauffiel. In addition to chastising Cauffiel, the editors at the paper said that black people in Johnstown were as frightened by the angry people there as they were of the mayor.

Dr. Jim Giesen, another history professor at Mississippi State, said holding on to labor was the first thing farmers tried to do when the boll weevil epidemic struck the South. The Great Migration had taken a toll on southern farming. And journalistic institutions in the South seized opportunities like the one in Johnstown to try to retain those workers.

"Southern newspaper editors would have jumped on those stories," Giesen said. "Whenever they popped up, they ran. They were trying to find anything they could do to make the North look more like the South and the South more like the North. They wanted to stem the tide of northern immigration."

The *Johnstown Democrat* carried an article from a South Carolina newspaper, *Columbia State*, called "Johnstown Repudiates Appomattox."

The newspaper said Cauffiel was in obvious defiance of the Constitution and announced that the city of Columbia never banned black people from coming in for the crime of one of their race. Then it took a more honest approach to its editorial:

> *In all seriousness, the policy adopted in Pennsylvania is menacing to the South. If Northern towns are to be permitted to drive Negroes out, that is equivalent to condemning them to stay in the South. It would be tantamount to a declaration by the North that the South shall never be free of Negroes.*
>
> *Moreover, if the North shall drive the Negroes back to the South, it will imply repudiation by the North of Mr. Lincoln's emancipation proclamation. Refusal to Negroes of the right to move and take up residence where they wish in the United States would be as much as to say that their re-enslavement where they now live would be ignored by the North.*

The *Columbia State* indicated that leaders from other towns in the North sympathized with Cauffiel's stance. It reported there were more members in the Ku Klux Klan in Indiana than anywhere else. The *State* then said President Coolidge and Secretary Bascom Slemp should do something and encouraged Senator Henry Cabot Lodge of Massachusetts to introduce legislation declaring action. Lodge had coauthored bills that had helped African Americans earlier in his career.

Another southern newspaper, the *Tampa Daily Times*, described the order and mayor as barbarous. It said African Americans had been wronged and betrayed in a house of supposed friends. The South, on the other hand, regretted to see them go, which is why states passed laws to restrain labor agents.

The *Marshall News Messenger* in Texas both reported on the Mexican government's action and analyzed what Cauffiel's action meant in the larger scheme of things going on in America. It claimed that black people belonged in the South, where they would be treated more equally.

Various publications put out information that black people shouldn't go north early in the twentieth century, according to Dr. Ralph Proctor.

"And they said if they were north, that they had to come back where they were loved," Dr. Proctor said. "*The Pittsburgh Courier* and black intellectuals said that was ridiculous. In some of those flyers, they were claiming the Northern winters were too cold. They told them it affected their brains and told them they would go insane. We didn't pay much attention to that. We knew that was propaganda and lies."

Black newspapers and southern agricultural leaders were always at odds during that time. One of the crimes the black press reported on was the lynching of black men in the South, according to Dr. William G. Jordan.

"The white or Southern lynchers would try to say that every lynching is a response to a horrible thing a black person did," Jordan said. "And the black press would give an accurate report. It was the start of 'fake news' if you will, in today's parlance. It was a battle over what the truth really is."

Northern newspapers noticed how southern plantation owners and journalists exploited the situation. The *Chicago Defender*, under Robert Sengstacke Abbott's direction, was an enthusiastic supporter of the Great Migration. Abbott, a remarkable figure in national journalism, felt it was an opportunity for African Americans to live free. He was born in 1868 to former slaves and raised in Savannah, Georgia. His dark complexion made him feel isolated not only within the white community but also within the black community, which he felt prized lighter complexions. He continually stressed the "aspirations, fears and grievances" of ordinary blacks while shying away from deep thinkers. When Abbott started his newspaper, he called it the *Defender* because he saw it as its duty to defend black people. For the first few months of the paper's existence, he lived on fish sandwiches and soda pop in order to pay for its printing. The paper caught on eventually. One of the reasons was that literacy increased among black people in the decades following the Civil War. More African Americans wanted to read things from their perspective. So black newspapers rose in popularity in northern industrial centers.

Abbott revolutionized black journalism by emulating the sensational yellow journalism style made famous by William Randolph Hearst and Joseph Pulitzer. Instead of putting community news on his page, he put out more exciting articles and content, including political cartoons lampooning racist government officials and acerbic editorials that pointed out and criticized black oppression. The headlines stuck out as well. Circulation soared. During the Johnstown affair, black newspapers across the country sensationalized how

A political cartoon that appeared in the *Chicago Defender* in October 1923 showed combatting images of what it was like in the South for black people. Southern newspapers and leaders said that black people were better off staying put because of the racism they would encounter in the North. The Johnstown incident was used as propaganda by southern cotton plantation owners to show life was better below the Mason-Dixon line. *Library of Congress, microfilm department.*

oppressive Joseph Cauffiel was and how much of an injustice his actions were. Nonetheless, in reading the headlines, it seems like the content and action were every bit as sensational as the portrayal black journalists gave it.

Abbott took southern newspapers to task for using the Johnstown incident as a chance to promote their region as more humane. "You will do well to pay attention to remarks made by Mayor Cauffiel of Johnstown, Pa. Our Southern dailies are making much of the reputed remarks of the mayor," read one editorial in the *Chicago Defender*. "'We told you so' is the attitude of white people South. 'Get rid of these NEW Negroes,' is the order of the mayor. Ponder that order."

Vann and his staff at the *Pittsburgh Courier* said the Johnstown incident was great news for southerners. Vann called for the immediate repudiation of Cauffiel from all northerners. He also called it extremely exceptional for black people to be ordered en masse out of a community.

"One Johnstowner will not serve to drive all Negroes back to the South," Vann wrote. "One swallow does not make a summer. But the telegram of President Wannamaker is information to the world that there is a lively bidding for Negro labor. May the laborer go to the highest and best bidder. And the while the bidders cry, the Negro should devote himself to sober thought."

Dr. Crew explained what went on at the time. "What you have in black newspapers is an encouragement to leave the South with all its discrimination and violence and look for something different," Crew said. "You can see that with the *Defender* and *Courier*. They're all saying to Southern African Americans that they need to leave. That's not what Southern agricultural leaders were saying. And so there are countervailing views on it between those groups."

Roscoe Simmons, Booker T. Washington's nephew, criticized Wannamaker in his weekly column. He had spent his childhood in Republican politics and was an aide for U.S. Senator Mark Hanna, a millionaire king of industry. Simmons went to work for the *Chicago Defender*, where he was one of the highest-paid and most popular columnists. He quoted Wannamaker saying that all industrious and law-abiding black people were wanted back South. But then he said people went north because of the power of the ballot, which was more powerful than anything that kept them South. Simmons wrote:

> *South Carolina colored people, settlers in the North or darting from pillar to post, would like to ask Mr. Wannamaker why weren't they entitled to "justice" before they got out of South Carolina....In Pennsylvania, so they say, they may not get justice, but they do get a hearing. Rattle dry bones in Abbeville, Mr. Wannamaker, and you will be told by a slain Negro, rich, respected, prosperous, that he was put off without counsel, justice or a hearing. "The white people South are the best friends the Negro has in America," is Mr. Wannamaker's opinion. Hardly any debate on that point.*
>
> *They ought to be, Negroes made them rich, lazy, gave them education, fed and clothed them, nursed the children, made the early fire, cooked the food, washed the dishes and wept over them when death came. Would you not think that enough to make our white people South friends to you? It ought to make them friends even to your children. Would you not think so, Mr. Wannamaker? What is the great love? That a man lay down his life for his friends? Who can deny that?*

CAUFFIEL'S EXPLANATIONS

At the mayor's office, a city executive received a telegram from the governor on September 19. Office attaches said the mayor's office would withhold contents of the telegram from public view for the moment because Cauffiel was absent and would not be available until the next day. The mayor's associates told reporters that they had no authority to talk for him and that any statement on the subject had to come from Cauffiel himself. When he got back, Cauffiel reiterated his former order and gave notice that those who had not complied with his order "better do so at once."

"I'm the one that's responsible for law and order, and I'm going to see that it's preserved here," he announced,

"All I've got to say now is: I want every Negro who comes under my order and who has not taken warning to get out of Johnstown by this time to pack up and get out. I am giving them fair warning. It's for their own good to get out."

By that time, three of the city's police officers involved in the shooting were dead.

"I tell you I fear the worst if the fourth man dies," he said.

Pressed on the subject, Cauffiel responded by walking away. He said the same thing the night of the order. He intimated that the public sentiment would be so aroused that Johnstown's black settlements "might go up that quick," snapping his fingers.

"It wasn't a case of politics. It was a case of law and order," he maintained. "I took a firm stand to combat and prevent further lawlessness among Negroes. I asked them to leave town only for their own safety. I'm sorry that some Negroes have not been able to view this thing in that light. Their safety is involved and yet they are disgruntled because I will not allow them to hold dances."

"Law and order in this community come before any political hopes I may have," he said. "I did my duty as I saw it. I have no apologies, no excuses, to make to anybody."

Cauffiel was unapologetic when he finally responded to the governor,

All the local papers had by and large turned against him. In an editorial called "Johnstown's Shame," the *Altoona Tribune* said that Cauffiel, and not the black residents, should be ordered out.

"Cauffiel as the German commandant of a captured French city or the chief burgess of an interior Georgia town might get away with an order like that, but it doesn't go in Pennsylvania," the *Tribune* wrote.

The *New York Amsterdam News* wrote about the incident in an editorial titled "The Cradle Is Rocking." It mentioned Ku Klux Klan activity in Tulsa, Oklahoma, before moving on to talk about Cauffiel: "Over in Johnstown, Pennsylvania, one man, Mayor Joseph Cauffiel, at one leap, bounded into the cradle and is trying to upset it. This libertine has issued an order that all Negroes who have not been residents of the city for at least seven years must leave, haste post haste. He knows full well that he has no such authority and that he is violating the Constitution of the land in issuing such an order, but is not worried by such trifles. Mayor Cauffiel must think that he is in Russia."

Though outsiders often deemed the banishment as a closed matter, Mayor Cauffiel continually opposed the newspapers and activists criticizing him. He insisted that the order, or request, was still in place. And for all intents and purposes, he intended on carrying it out.

"I have not retracted. This is no place for the Negro," Cauffiel said. "I know that law-abiding citizens of this community back me up in my stand. I wish some of these society officials and newspaper writers that are yelling their heads off because I took the only means to save hundreds of people from mob action and consequent results, would come here and spend a week in Franklin, a Negro colony, just outside the city limits. It's a hellhole of wickedness, with dens of dope peddlers, moonshine, bootleggers and rows of houses of prostitution. We'll have nothing like that in Johnstown as long as I am mayor. They are all out of Rosedale, and I wish I had the power to clean out the Franklin borough district."

Black journalists focused on Johnstown and Mayor Cauffiel. Roscoe Simmons wrote about Johnstown in his column "The Week," which appeared in the *Chicago Defender*. He urged black people to be accountable for their actions to reduce the number of crimes that could trigger something like the Johnstown incident.

"Trouble broke out in Johnstown during the absence of the mayor," Simmons said. "Colored men, maybe one or two fresh from the South, were too handy with guns. Much handier in Johnstown than below the Mason and Dixon line.

"Bravery may pick its ground, courage never. Your preachers North might preach from the text, 'Thou shalt not kill,' and tell newcomers in toting guns and killing people who haven't done anything to them, they make it hard on those who want to be somebody."

Simmons commented that thousands of black men seemed bent on proving that they were troublemakers.

"Razor toting and gun carrying must be cut out in the North," Simmons said. "You got that stuff from white people South. Nobody likes a tough bad race. If you can't behave yourselves in your new home, among people who wish you well, who give you a helping hand, overlook many, many shortcomings, go back home."

Within black journalism at the time, there was a wide array of perspectives. In New York, Chandler Owen wrote from a radical viewpoint. Simmons was much more conservative. And Vann, in Pittsburgh, was middle-of-the-road. He carried writing from black writers of all political viewpoints.

In addition to the *Courier*, the *Messenger* and the *Chicago Defender*, other African American newspapers included the *Chicago Bee*, the *Richmond Planet*, the *Baltimore Afro-American*, the *New York Amsterdam News* and dozens of others. The black media had its own wire service, the Chicago-based Associated Negro Press, which provided reports to newspapers from correspondents throughout the country. There were also a variety of specialized black publications produced by prominent black leaders.

Their growing power bases in northern cities like Chicago and Pittsburgh showed they spoke to the minds of new arrivals. Circulation of those newspapers climbed throughout the entirety of the Great Migration. Their power increased correspondingly. Some failed because advertisers wouldn't place spots in their papers.

Often articles in black newspapers contained analysis that wasn't found elsewhere. That was especially true during the Rosedale incident, in which the black perspective wasn't given much space or text by white reporters, who seemed focused instead on the actions of the white mayor and other public officials. The coverage given to Cauffiel by the black press indicated how the activists perceived him.

The *New York Age*, a black weekly, also covered the Johnstown affair. Fred R. Moore, a political activist and journalist who was born to a slave mother and white father in Virginia, helmed the publication. In the early part of the century, the *Age* was the most widely read black newspaper in the country. He promoted black capitalism, Republican politics and the cultural accomplishments for blacks. Moore helped found the National League on Urban Conditions in New York City, which later became the National Urban League. Most black newspapers in the United States were weeklies. Most thought that it would be difficult to fill a daily newspaper with news that dealt with African Americans. Week after week, during the month of September 1923, the black newspapers carried news and thoughts on the people and mayor of Johnstown. Moore and his staff were unsparing in their criticism of Cauffiel in an editorial titled "Is This Within the Law?"

It read, in part: "A decree of exile used to be a favorite device exercised by dictators in some of the South American countries to get rid of obnoxious citizens and foreigners, but we did not know that it was recognized as a legal punishment or procedure under the laws of any State in the Union."

The black papers had been the driving force behind Cauffiel's disgrace. They carried the story on front pages throughout the ordeal, and they compelled larger newspapers such as the *New York Times*, *Los Angeles Times* and others to follow suit. It was a testament to how powerful they had become in America because of their ability to comfort the afflicted and afflict the comfortable. The country was not allowed to forget injustices. Because of them, activists across the country rallied to fight against perpetrators of injustice. Would Cauffiel have lost the election without the attention focused on him by the black newspapers? It's difficult to say. But because black people had a voice, a way to know what was happening to them in towns and cities big and small, they forced action. Cauffiel's defeat showed the power of the press and an important political evolution in America. White newspapers no longer solely dictated what the country should pay attention to. And they paid attention to Johnstown and Cauffiel as a result.

Dr. William G. Jordan said that the early 1920s were a bad time for black equality. Some described it as the nadir for the civil rights struggle. But the importance of African American journalists can't be overstated in preserving and cultivating the convictions needed in the decades ahead.

"There was not much progress being made," Jordan said.

And yet there were these institutions still fighting for rights. And the black press was the most important of them, even more than the church. The black press was a much more important force in this earlier period, and it played a significant role in keeping the fires for black freedom alive when it seemed like it wasn't going anywhere. In fact it seemed like it was going backwards. They kept it going until the time was more ripe for progress. The black community had maintained a consciousness. They didn't give up.

STATE INVESTIGATION

Pinchot finally acted after reading all of the telegrams while in Milford, Pennsylvania, where he had been the entire time. On September 21, Pennsylvania attorney general George W. Woodruff announced that Governor Pinchot ordered a thorough investigation of the Johnstown incident following the onslaught of telegrams. Deputy Attorney General John N. English went to Johnstown.

Cauffiel hedged following the announcement. He insisted that the order was never formal. He had merely "advised" black people for their own safety and the good of Johnstown to leave. Thousands were gone by that time. By one account, most went west toward Pittsburgh. Cauffiel said he was confident the governor wouldn't punish him.

"I sent Governor Pinchot a complete account of conditions here and he should have the real facts before him now," Cauffiel protested. "I have every confidence in the world that I will not hear from him again on the matter. Immediately following the Negro outbreak in which police officers were killed, sentiment in Johnstown was such that I could not guarantee protection to Negroes and Mexican classes, and the only recourse I had was to send them out of town."

The NAACP announced that it would push the case against the mayor to the fullest extent. The national office of the NAACP secured the services of attorney George H. White Jr. of Pittsburgh.[56] White rapidly gathered evidence that the NAACP leaders hoped would form the basis for impeachment proceedings against Cauffiel. They felt it was possible given that the Mexican government, through its embassy, had joined the NAACP in moving against the mayor. James Weldon Johnson, in commenting on the importance of the case and the far-reaching effect of the successful fight against Mayor Cauffiel, said that his high-handed and arbitrary action had received a just rebuke:

> *The NAACP regards the outcome of the Johnstown affair as having a far-reaching effect upon the vital interests not only of the Negroes concerned but of all workers. If Mayor Cauffiel had been allowed without rebuke to order the wholesale deportation of 2,000 Negroes regardless of innocence or guilt of the individuals concerned, he or any other mayor might have issued a similar order regarding colored people or any other group whenever any individual committed or was accused of committing a crime.*
>
> *The decisive repudiation of the mayor's action nips in the bud similar attempts which would affect seriously the migration of Negroes from the mob-ridden South. Southern white newspapers would have played up eternally the incident in such fashion as to have deterred colored people from seeking greater freedom in the North. Having seen what happened to Mayor Cauffiel, other mayors or public officials will hesitate a long time before trying any similar tactics.*

At the Cambria Iron Works, where many area African Americans still worked, no statement was available aside from that the company had ceased bringing to Johnstown additional black laborers from the South.

Cauffiel denied that the police were used to compel blacks to quit Johnstown. "I have done nothing more than use that power I have as mayor of this city to protect white residents and Negroes, and I do not fear investigation by the governor or anybody else," he said.

The *Johnstown Democrat* blasted Cauffiel for characterizing his order as a piece of advice. It quoted his original story and said the words spoke for themselves. "This does not sound much like a request," the *Democrat* commented. "It would seem to be in the nature of a command. It was at least so interpreted by the public and by the Negroes themselves. And it has stirred Negroes from all over the country to a protest which has reached Gov. Pinchot and which has drawn from the governor a promise that he will investigate the matter with a view to protecting colored people in their rights as American citizens.

"Just what course the governor will pursue in case he reached the conclusion that those rights have been summarily invaded by Mayor Cauffiel we do not pretend to know. But inasmuch as there are a good many thousands of colored voters in Pennsylvania, it is conceivable that a governor who is looking higher might consider it to his advantage to discipline a mayor whom he may regard as having overstepped proper bounds in declaring that the 'Negroes must go back from where they came.'"

Pinchot had two possible options. He could use the commonwealth's military force to prevent the deportation of blacks and Mexicans from Johnstown. Or he could call a special session of the state senate and have the mayor deposed. Under the state constitution, the governor with the consent of two-thirds of the senate could remove a city's mayor.

When English arrived, the mayor told newspaper reporters that "peace and order reign in Johnstown again, and this incident is closed."

English spent just a few days in Johnstown and interviewed a number of people, including the district attorney, the chief of police, Mayor Cauffiel, local religious leaders and residents of Rosedale. He sifted through local newspaper coverage, of which the *Johnstown Democrat* was of more use. He told reporters upon his departure that he felt assured by city and county officials as well as citizens of Johnstown that, regardless of creed or color, they would be given the same constitutional rights in the administration of justice.[57] He returned to Harrisburg to file his report. As for the official investigation results, at the suggestion of Governor Pinchot, the Pennsylvania Department of Justice announced there was little foundation to the charge that Cauffiel ordered African Americans and Mexicans out in an official capacity.

Police were absolved of any wrongdoing. They did not attempt to carry out the deportation, according to English. But the report also said that Cauffiel tried to enforce his order through sentencing at police court. English estimated the number of people who left to be somewhere in the range of three hundred to one thousand, far below most other estimates.

English told newspaper reporters that magistrates and mayors who held their own police hearings told tramps and other undesirables to leave a city within an hour often, but their order was never general. Telling the defendants to do so never held any legal power, but that didn't mean the person charged with the crime was aware of that. Pinchot said the investigation concluded that there was nothing to indicate that Cauffiel had overstepped his authority. Pinchot sent a letter censuring Cauffiel's conduct and admonished him to observe the law.

English said people left because they felt the mayor's attitude and actions would result in actual enforcement from the police or mayor. It was understood as an order that could and would be enforced. They feared that the Ku Klux Klan or mobs would attack them and destroy their homes.

There was a flaw in English's report. It failed to mention that Cauffiel employed private detectives to do his bidding. That was a big problem insofar as the allegations that black people had been marched out at gunpoint. While the police department may not have done so, it is unclear whether Cauffiel told his own private officers to march through Rosedale and other black communities to tell the locals there to leave with the threat of guns.

Though official action had been taken, the fallout over the order continued to be felt, with criticism from across the country coming toward the small city to the east of Pittsburgh. Pinchot received praise in the *Baltimore Afro-American*, which said he was running true to form:

> *Although Theodore Roosevelt is dead, his soul goes marching on. He proclaims civic righteousness for the state of Pennsylvania and for all of the inhabitants thereof. When appealed to by the NAACP to restrain the lawless and outrageous procedure of the mayor of Johnstown, he responded with true American spirit and courage.*
>
> *The promise to exhaust all of the constitutional powers of the state to guarantee to all citizens their constitutional rights. Pinchot says what he means, and means what he says. Capital and labor both understand this and the lawless mayor of Johnstown will be made to understand it. This country stands sadly in need of righteousness and courage, in high places. If this nation does not destroy lawlessness, lawlessness will destroy the nation.*

Criticism of Cauffiel came from as far away as Montana. The *Great Falls Tribune* criticized him in an editorial:

> *One is inclined to ask "of what meat does this our Caesar feed that he hath grown so great?" Who gave him power to expel American citizens who have resided there less than seven years because their complexion is dark, or even Mexican citizens who are aliens if they have been behaving themselves properly? If he can compel every Negro who enters his city to visit the office of the mayor and chief of police and register there, he can compel every white citizen to do the same.*

The *Los Angeles Times* described the order as un-American and compared Cauffiel to Hamlet, who believes that the times are out of joint and that Providence had appointed him to set them right. Cauffiel, however, didn't lament that fact like Hamlet, but exulted in it. The *Times* blasted him for being on vacation while the shooting happened:

> *Being a mighty protagonist of law and order, justice and right, the official called forth his cohorts and ran 2,000 of the wretched newcomers out of town. More are to follow, only those Negroes who can prove several years' continuous residence within the delightful walls of Johnstown being permitted to remain. Those who were given no time to arrange their small affairs or make provision as to where they would go. The mayor believed that they should be punished for their temerity in thinking, because they were born in America, they had a right to migrate to any town they chose in search of better employment.*

The paper added that no one supported Cauffiel—aside from the Klan:

> *With the exception of the Ku Klux Klan, which held a grand celebration in Johnstown in honor of the glad event, that they believed was an added embellishment to the noble edifice of liberty and freedom, Americans have erected through generations of devotion to the ideal of a square deal to all. Such actions as these postpone further into the future the day of a rational solution of the colored problem, and arouse bitterness and hate in the hearts of thousands of peaceful, law-abiding Negroes.*

The Johnstown Democrat commented on it as well: "The Negroes who have come to Johnstown in search of employment may not all of them be of the most desirable class. But until they have committed some overt act they are entitled to the same freedom of movement and the same protection as whites who come hither to work in our various industries."

The Chicago Defender again criticized Cauffiel in an editorial published on September 22, "Getting Rough":

> *Someone needs to take Joseph Cauffiel, mayor of Johnstown, Pa., aside and inform him gently but firmly that the days of czardom are in the dim and distant past and that he was elected by and is a servant of all citizens of the little burg over which he is temporarily presiding. His edict that all colored people must immediately leave under (threat) of being driven out by the police would be laughable were it not for the fact that any attempt to force such an unlawful order will unquestionably result in a miniature race war and the sacrificing of many innocent lives.*

The *Defender* pointed out that Cauffiel had threatened to drive black people out by gun:

> *All of this wild outburst because a little nest of dope joints and moonshine stills furnished bad men enough to shoot several police officers fatally. Bad characters are the same whether they be black or white and there are more white ones than black ones for the reason that their group is about eight times larger in this country. Surely the police of Johnstown have found white dope fiends and white bootleggers. Why hasn't the mayor ordered all white people to be driven from the town at the point of gun?*

The *Defender* said Cauffiel had gone a step too far. And his action was bitter, unreasonable and unlawful, and it would eventually render him an ineffective executive.

> *It is regrettable that such things should take place in any part of our country, but it was least expected from Pennsylvania. Mayor Cauffiel will find that it doesn't pay to get rough and in the near future when he can class himself as a political has-been, he will have ample time to reflect on his rash order that made him the laughingstock of the whole country.*

James Weldon Johnson credited Pinchot and the voters of Johnstown. "Again, had the attempt to deport the Negroes and Mexicans been successful, invitations would have been extended by that success to the Ku Klux Klan and the mob to murder and hurry Negro citizens wherever they chose in the North," he said. "Governor Pinchot acted promptly and vigorously and deserves a sincere thanks and praise of all colored people and fair-minded people. Also the citizens of Johnstown are to be thanked for their prompt and decisive repudiation of Mayor Cauffiel at the polls."

After the publicity died down, the *Buffalo American* acknowledged the importance of the NAACP in ensuring the rights of all people of color. It brought attention to terrible things that happened to their race across the country, including in Johnstown. The paper called Cauffiel's order inhuman:

> *We, repeat, we, the Negroes of America, should awake to the necessity of a more liberal support of this organization. There should be no less than a paying membership of three hundred thousand. Wonderful things have been done with the limited amount of money put into the hands of these men and women with which they might fight our battles in the courts.*

What might be done if given the support which they deserve and we owe? Let the pulpit and the press be the means of arousing that self-interest in the race that may bring the needed support to this organization, for the men and women who compose it are working for this race, and not for themselves. Of this, there is no room for doubt. Their only reward comes from a consciousness of having labored in behalf of justice and right. When a case is won against injustice and wrong, their rejoicing is equal to our own.

AFTERMATH

Two thousand enthusiastic black men and women, many of them from neighboring states, packed the Peoples Gospel Tabernacle along Hemans Street, near Centre Avenue, in Pittsburgh, to hear Marcus Garvey, founder and leader of the Universal Negro Improvement Association, at the beginning of October.

Garvey pointed to the Johnstown incident as what black people might expect in the future, declaring that economic conditions caused it. He characterized Cauffiel as a man who probably did not hate black people but was willing to drive them from the city to appease public opinion. Garvey denounced the mayor, police and white workers of Johnstown.

"The unemployed whites were waiting for an opportunity to run the employed and unemployed Negroes out of town, so as to brighten their prospects for employment," Garvey said of the situation. "The opportunity presented itself when two policemen were shot in one of the labor districts of the city. It is apparent that the white labor leaders seized upon the opportunity of getting the mayor to take immediate action, which he did not fail to do. The result was that thousands of Negroes were driven out of town by the order of Mayor Joseph Cauffiel."

Garvey posited that the same thing might happen elsewhere. "We will find other mayors all over the United States making similar declarations, and in a short while, except where the Negro has created for himself a haven of refuge, he will become the unfortunate man without a country and without a shelter."[58]

What happened to the people who left Johnstown remains a mystery, even a century later. Frightened, penniless and at a loss, black families of men, women, children and old folk gathered up a few belongings and set out on the highway or on railroads, not knowing where they were going to go.

The *Literary Digest* weighed in on the issue in an article for the October 6, 1923 edition titled "Johnstown's Flood of Negro Labor":

> *Not since the Johnstown Flood has that Pennsylvania city been so much in the public eye as it has been since its mayor warned most of the negro residents, "for their own safety and the safety of the public," to leave the city at once, following a riot in a negro colony in which the instigator and three white policemen were killed, and two others seriously wounded.*

Racial cleansings were common during that time. They mostly occurred in the North but also took place below the Mason-Dixon line. The general indifference to the people banished from Johnstown is troubling. The coverage of their struggle virtually disappeared after the initial hoopla, and even when it did become a topic of discussion, it was generally dismissed quickly.

"So a few months ago Mayor Cauffiel of Johnstown found himself forced to 'deport' a great number of negro families whose presence was resented by white workers," read one editorial in Philadelphia's *Evening Public Ledger* in 1924. "The negroes had moved northward in the labor exodus of the last two years. Where they finally went no one seems to know or care."

Bruce G. Haselrig, a member of First Cambria Zion AME Church and a local black leader in modern-day Johnstown, spoke to a few people who were there at the time. "A lot of people did leave. They didn't stay. I met some relatives who passed through here when that happened," Haselrig told the *Somerset Daily American*. "A lot ended up in Buffalo and Cleveland. But because of the mayor, with his order to leave, they did. I went to a couple of funerals in Buffalo with some Hemphills and Richardsons who came from the South, and they said they should keep going. Our black population would have been much bigger if that wouldn't have happened."[59]

The Reverend James Johnson, the current pastor of First Cambria Zion AME Church, said that people were reluctant to talk about incidents like that during the decades that followed because they feared retribution: "Especially back when it took place, African Americans in many circles… we weren't considered human. We didn't have any real rights. And it was the time of Jim Crow law. If you spoke up, it could be a death sentence.

People were reluctant to speak up individually. That's what gave so much power to the church. People could come together collectively and have much more safety."

Marco Williams, a filmmaker who produced *Banished*, a critically acclaimed documentary about racial expulsions, said that there is a dark aspect to Americans not knowing this part of history or having it taught to them in schools.

"Amnesia means something we knew or something we forgot," Williams said. "But I think it's a little more willful. I think they reflect plain and simple that it's underreported or not told as part of history. It is an extension of white supremacy."

Another Pennsylvania town attempted to banish its black population a month after the exodus from Johnstown. This time it was in Stowe. A "go" order was issued to "every Negro to pack up his belongings and move elsewhere within 24 hours" by a committee of more than two hundred men. The order followed the murder of Thomas Rowland, a seventy-five-year-old white man, and the wounding of his eleven-year-old granddaughter, Edith Colter, by a black man. The township had been home to a number of African Americans for several years, and many of them were determined to stay. James Weldon Johnson sent Pinchot a letter again registering the NAACP's protest.

"It is again our unpleasant duty to call to your attention another attempt to drive Negroes regardless of innocence or guilt from a Pennsylvania town because of a crime charged to one colored man," Johnson said in a telegram. "This incident arose in the Stowe Township district, and press dispatches report that many Negroes have left there after being ordered to get out by a Vigilance Committee on the night of October 9 [1923]. May we again request of you action to prevent injustice to these colored citizens and protection of their civil rights."

After the Stowe incident, southern newspapers again blasted northerners' treatment of black people. Journalists commented that it showed what the people of Pennsylvania really thought of African Americans. In Alabama, the *Clarke County Democrat* explained what it thought of the region:

> *It also shows that human nature is pretty much the same the country over, and that like reactions will be caused by like conditions and circumstances. Where work is not plentiful white men often take strenuous means to express their resentment at being supplanted in their jobs of members of a different race. The fundamental difference between the North and South in this*

respect is that in the South the Negro is not brought into that close and direct
competition with the whites that largely prevails in Northern plants.

It added that both races understood their rights in the South and there
were rarely race clashes. The newspaper said that both black people and the
agents who recruited them would realize that African Americans were not
meant to be in the North.

Soon after the Johnstown incident, a similar exodus occurred in South
Bend, Indiana, where 1,000 to 1,500 black residents reportedly left within
twenty-four hours after a well-known black citizen received a threatening
letter. The *Baltimore Afro-American* wrote about what it meant for racial
relations and tried to give readers an insight into whether the North or the
South was better to black people:

> *The drastic efforts of the authorities of these two Northern cities to rid*
> *themselves of the Negro element because of a few undesirables of that race*
> *have led to a number of Southern journals to repeat their old-time platitude*
> *that the South is the best place of the black man. They tell us that the South*
> *understands the Negro and that the Southern people are his best friends.*

Whenever there was an outbreak of racial hatred up North, white
southerners were quick to remind black people of their hospitality, as the
Baltimore Afro-American editorial put it.

"There is much abuse of the word friendship," the paper continued.
"Cicero tells that friendship can only exist between equals. So long as the
South looks upon the Negro as an inferior order of being, there can not exist
the true meaning and spirit of friendship between the races."

The newspaper said southerners looked at black people as they would a
horse or a faithful dog, but not as a man or person:

> *It is doubtless true that the South may treat the Negro more kindly in*
> *some respects than the North. It may put up with his numerous faults*
> *and shortcomings; but this is mainly because it does not expect any high*
> *manifestation of human qualities from such forbidden source.*
>
> *On the other hand the North may seem hard and severe in its exactions,*
> *and may become impatient even to the point of rash action over many of the*
> *obvious imperfections of the Negro newcomers, but this is merely because*
> *it upholds a higher standard of conduct and efficiency and requires every*
> *citizen, white or black, to live up to this higher standard.*

When Dr. S.P.W. Drew, a black welfare worker, came to Altoona for several days in late September 1923 as part of his work with the White Cross Free Labor Bureau, he discussed the Johnstown exodus. He characterized it as "a disgrace to Pennsylvania."

His organization placed southern African Americans in northern communities for work to which they were fitted. Drew went to Johnstown and tried to see the mayor to get an explanation. He also wanted to talk to Governor Pinchot. Drew's agency was responsible for establishing part of Johnstown's black settlements. A number of the men he brought purchased their own homes.

"The Southern states are making the most of the Johnstown affair," Drew said. "The story is being broadcast throughout the South as propaganda by those who are seeking to stop Negroes from moving to states where they can secure employment at better wages and under better conditions. They say that the North doesn't want the Negroes and will drive them out. The story is worth $100,000 to them as propaganda.

"If there was a crime committed at Johnstown by Negroes, why wreak punishment on all people of the race? To drive people of any race from a town is against the Constitution and is a disgrace to the memory of the Pennsylvanians who fought for liberty."

Following the exodus of black labor, Bethlehem Steel ran at 70 percent capacity.

As for the officers involved in the shooting, Captain Otto Fink died that November. He left behind a widow and four children.

Black people faced prejudice in Johnstown in the months following the banishment. When black residents tried to establish a church in the heart of one of Johnstown's best residential sections, prominent business leaders in the community condemned them. M.D. Bearer, treasurer of Title, Trust & Guarantee Company, along with James C. Griffith, cashier of the First National Bank, and William H. Thomas, a businessman, issued a statement that called on all citizens of the city not to support the congregation through contributions or other means. They accused the pastor, the Reverend C.A. Brady, of misrepresenting his attempt to collect $40,000 to pay for the church's construction.

They pointed out that the location of the black church was not far from sections of the city in which black people predominantly resided. They would gladly support the construction of a church in Rosedale, Franklin or Conemaugh. The three men thought the church's presence in those communities would deter violence toward police.

In December 1923, with Cauffiel still a magistrate, police arrested twenty-five black people in a raid of an alleged gambling den. Each was fined fifty dollars or faced sixty days in jail and ordered, upon payment of fine or release from jail, to get below the Mason-Dixon line. Cauffiel continued to use the tactic long after the hullabaloo died down.

When Cauffiel told Johnstown residents that he had tired of political life and planned to retire on January 1, 1924, the *Pittsburgh Courier* took it as a last chance to remind citizens of the kind of man he was. The paper pointed out that he was a defendant in seventy-four lawsuits aggregating $1 million.

"Out he goes—he has gone, but does not know it. Seemingly the people made the decision for him before he made it. Then along came this political Poe. One should retire before he is retired. This is the potent lesson of history. Yet as Hegel said: 'We know from history that men never learn anything from history.'"

Cauffiel didn't hold true to his promise to retire on New Year's Day. In the next year, shortly after a gambling ring had been banished, Cauffiel addressed twenty African Americans who came into police court after they had been arrested in a poolroom.

"Go back South and don't show your face again above the Mason-Dixon line," Cauffiel told them in January 1924.

Cauffiel was in and out of trouble for the remainder of his life. He was frequently accused of corruption. Later in the 1920s, he was elected mayor once more, as an independent candidate. Following another controversial incident in which two policemen were shot and fatally wounded by a black man in 1927, Cauffiel's reelection strategy did not focus on exploiting that situation for political gain, likely because of his experience four years earlier with the negative publicity that came from taking an anti-black stance. But Cauffiel's reputation as being hard on black criminals couldn't have hurt his reelection bid in an environment in which anger once again focused on the African American population. Following the election, the *Johnstown Democrat* raised the issue of voter fraud after suspicious results came in from various ballot boxes throughout the vicinity.

During his last term, he was convicted of extortion, perjury and a misdemeanor, removed from office and sentenced to two years in the county jail at Ebensburg. At Cauffiel's trial, the gambler who ran the illicit establishment said he gave the mayor 40 percent of his receipts after expenses. The prosecutor said police never raided the place during Cauffiel's final term. Cauffiel served eighteen months before Governor Pinchot pardoned him. While in prison, the former mayor became ill. When he got out, he

MAYOR, IN JAIL, CLAIMS AUTHORITY

Mayor Joseph Cauffiel of Johnstown (left), shown with Night Warden T. M. Means in the Cambria County jail at Ebensburg, where His Honor yesterday began serving a two-year sentence. Cauffiel claims he still retains the powers of his office.

Johnstown mayor Joseph Cauffiel was indicted and sent to prison following the end of his political career in the 1920s. Cauffiel was sued and charged numerous times for his unethical and corrupt behavior while in office and in business. This photo appeared in the *Pittsburgh Press* in December 1929. *Newspapers.com.*

returned to his residence in the seventeenth ward of Johnstown. Cauffiel had been deathly sick, but he had been able to get around for a few months. He was under the care of a local physician and a specialist from Baltimore. Cauffiel died in July 1932 at his home in Moxham. He was sixty-three years old. He was buried on a windswept hill in nearby Jenner Township.

Afterward, Johnstown City Hall was draped in mourning for thirty days as a tribute to Cauffiel's memory. Members of the city council attended his funeral, and they sent a floral offering to his house and a letter of sympathy to his bereaved wife and family.

Upon Cauffiel's death, the Reverend Philip Bohan, longtime pastor of St. Patrick's Catholic Church in Moxham, praised Cauffiel in a statement sent to his parsonage. He called Cauffiel a friend of the poor and praised his character and morality.

"Few men in public life had more friends and less enemies than Johnstown's deceased mayor," he said. "His countless friends and admirers will mourn his loss and will dwell on the many admirable qualities that marked his life.

Johnstown City Hall in the early part of the twentieth century. Mayor Joseph Cauffiel's office was located in the building, and many of his operatives in the community spread his message to reporters during the Rosedale ordeal. *Courtesy of the Johnstown Area Heritage Association.*

A man who rose from a country boy to position and affluence, especially during times of upheaval, he deserved congratulations."

The *Johnstown Democrat* reminded readers that the paper had been squarely behind Cauffiel in his fight against public utilities:

> *More than a person, he was a personality. For twelve years, he was a dominant factor in this city. Wherever his political life ran, there were those thousands who followed him with unquestioning devotion. If Joseph Cauffiel had sought election as mayor of Johnstown for a fourth term, he would have been elected.*
>
> *Men who fight bear wounds and make enemies. But they also bind people to them. As between those who denounce and those who praise—an infinitely just judge eventually intervenes. Today this column neither denounces nor praises—except to say this. Joseph Cauffiel so thoroughly stood the test of personal association that the final comment made for and on behalf of the publisher of this paper is that for twenty years Joseph Cauffiel was a kind, helpful, considerate neighbor and "was splendid in his home." Epitaph enough for any man.*

In 1938, a legislative commission in Pennsylvania issued a report that found many court evils within the state. Investigators spent $50,000 looking into the issue. Forty-eight of the sixty-seven counties in Pennsylvania held 135 hearings. It painted a picture of malpractice in those courts, high and low, as well as in other channels of legal procedure. One of the pushes the commission made was to eliminate the mayor's court in Philadelphia. It raised the issue after the mayor there brought unnecessary newspaper publicity because of his administration of criminal justice. In the years that followed, there was an effort to abolish mayor's courts because they were a violation of the separation of powers principle. In 1968, the Pennsylvania legislature adopted a new constitution that stipulates that no member of the statewide judiciary shall hold political office or public appointment for which he or she receives compensation—nor will he or she hold office in a political party or organization.

Gifford Pinchot served in office until 1927, but the people reelected him as Pennsylvania governor in 1931 after an intervening term by another man. Throughout his time in office, he showed a deep concern for the disempowered and the rights of minorities. He appointed a black man to the State Athletic Commission, which was the highest position ever held by an African American in the Pennsylvania state government. He vigorously fought against anything that he thought denied constitutional rights. Still, Pinchot didn't move to impeach Cauffiel. Instead, he ordered an investigation and reassured the NAACP. And yet the mayor remained in his position until the next year. But in the context of his time, Gifford Pinchot was a progressive champion of the underprivileged, including African Americans.

Toward the end of 1923, civil rights leaders said that the response to the Johnstown incident was a sign of racial progress. In December, the Federal Council of Churches had a presentation by its Commission on Race Relations. Dr. George E. Haynes of New York spoke at the event.

So did Hallie Paxson Winsborough, who was the St. Louis superintendent of the Women's Auxiliary of the Presbyterian Church in the United States. She asserted that the Ku Klux Klan was the greatest menace to racial peace in the country.

"While persecuting the race from which our Master came, they have adopted the cross as their symbol and saddest of all have enlisted among their followers thousands of those who profess to be followers of the lowly Nazarene who came to bring peace to the world and who called all men His Brethren," she said. "This organization is reaching its terrible tentacles into every State in the Union. The time for inaction has passed. If this monster is to be crushed, it may be done by the Christian people of America."

In the decade following the exodus, Klan membership in Cambria County declined. It peaked shortly after 1923, yet remaining members were able to undertake ostentatious cross burnings and mass gatherings. At some initiations, four thousand people from Cambria and neighboring Somerset and Westmoreland Counties came. But eventually the Klan lost its appeal. The cross burnings attracted fewer volunteers. Imprisoned Klansmen were not seen as martyrs anymore. The organization's violent reputation hurt its recruitment efforts. By 1929, the Johnstown Klavern's membership had dwindled to a few people.

The *Altoona Tribune* wrote a story in November about African Americans traveling back to the South in large numbers. People watching trains in Altoona for months had noted the large number of black passengers on the night trains passing through the Mountain City, with one hundred travelers going eastward to every individual moving west. Many were homesick and didn't like the cold northern temperatures.

"Out of a job" was given as the main reason for going back. Large industries in western Pennsylvania and eastern Ohio fired men in large numbers. They were disproportionately black workers.

People saw whole families on the trains, with bag and baggage, testifying mutely to the fact that they shook the dust from their feet of the great North, which offered such great and glowing inducements during spring and summer but proved to be inhospitable in the winter. The winter months gave meager profit for those who returned.

Some prominent scholars, including Josephus Daniels, secretary of the navy in Woodrow Wilson's cabinet, commented on the phenomenon. Daniels was a supporter of southern plantation owners and believed the southern white man was the black man's best friend. "The real reason that carried Negroes north was economic and that is the reason why the movement southward is now seen. It will increase as the snow falls. Still quite a few will remain."

Daniels commented on Johnstown specifically: "After the talk by the mayor, it may be certain that the black belt will not permanently be shifted from Mississippi to Johnstown, Pa. That city does not seem to wish a flood of Negro citizens."

Southern newspaper editors at leading papers in six of the states in the region issued a collective statement asking for mutual helpfulness and cooperation between the white and black races in the South for equal education, equality before the law and the abatement of mob violence. Some said it reflected the attitude of the southern press.

"In the attainment and maintenance of improved interracial relations in our Southern states we believe that a policy of cooperation between the more thoughtful of both races is fundamental, this being the antithesis of antagonism and polemic discussion," the statement read. "Mutual helpfulness between whites and blacks should be encouraged, the better element, of both races, striving by precept and example to impress the interdependence of peoples living side by side, yet apart."

The white power structure in the South used newspapers as an instrument to keep its influence. The tone was reactionary to any northern attempt to bring integration in that region. Often the newspapers incited violence, rather than quelling it. The separate but equal manner of living prevailed in the South until it ended with the civil rights movement of the 1950s and 1960s.

Most weren't deterred from coming north or remaining there. The migration created a contagious feeling that it was somehow better—or at least held the promise to be. Both historically and economically, the North felt like it was friendlier to black people. Newspapers within that community seemed to say as much. Railway stations were congested with people who wanted to come, even after the Rosedale affair and a number of other incidents used by southern newspapers to try to keep them in the region.

"The entire Negro population of the South seems to be deeply affected," read one article in the *Age-Herald* during the early years of the Migration. "The fact that many Negroes who went north without sufficient funds and without clothing to keep them warm have suffered severely and have died in large numbers, has not checked the tide leaving the South. It was expected that the Negroes would come back, sorry that they ever left, but comparatively few have returned. With the approach of warmer weather the number going north will increase."[60]

When they came, they faced prejudice, and it increased in proportion to the number who resettled in the North. John Owen speculated for the *Baltimore Sun* that similar situations to the Rosedale incident could happen elsewhere.

"Because every town has people of bad judgment, sometimes in official life, sometimes on the streets, sometimes in organizations like the Klan, there is reason to fear that Johnstown's troubles are the forerunner of troubles in other Northern industrial communities in which great numbers of Negroes, good and bad, are being sent from the South," Owen said. "The process of adjusting these Negroes to Northern communities gives men of 'bad judgment' unusual opportunities for self-expression."[61]

The black people who came north grew in power. There was a growing race consciousness with groups, churches and other organizations formed in the North. Among people in Johnstown, for years following the Rosedale incident, there is and has been a reluctance to talk about what happened. Most of the black population at the time left as a result of the order. And when asked about it nearly a century later, some white residents don't even know about it or that it was a part of local history.

In the years that followed the Rosedale incident, leaders within the black community lobbied for newspapers to adopt a different policy when reporting on African American crime. In 1947, NAACP president Burrell Johnson said that black people suffered the most separation and consequently were regarded as second-class citizens.

"Use the same standard of evaluation on each man and forget his color or the church he attends," Johnson exhorted.

By that year, the membership in the Johnstown branch had soared to 647 people, according to an article compiled in a folder at the Library of Congress. They fought issues such as school segregation and the inability to access local libraries.

The next few decades were filled with fights for fair housing and quality education for black children. As the national civil rights movement became increasingly the focus of the country's attention, the Johnstown branch of the NAACP took note and pushed for equality. It was a tumultuous time in the nation's history, with African Americans and white people hopping on buses to take "Freedom Rides" into the South to desegregate lunch counters.

White people in the North were horrified by newspaper accounts and photos of one of those buses being set on fire and of people being dragged and beaten by mobs. One of the challenges faced by local civil rights leaders was making white residents aware that some of the worst racism in the United States was in the northern industrial centers of Johnstown, Pittsburgh, Detroit and Cleveland.

Black people had a difficult time buying homes in the North. In one letter that Johnstown NAACP president Frank D. Davis wrote to the national headquarters in New York in 1956, he revealed that he had arranged for a white man to act as a "dummy" in order to purchase a home for a black couple that couldn't get it on their own.

"Judging from their experience at that time and from current real estate and financing practices in Johnstown, it seems likely they would have trouble getting mortgage money locally for a property obtained now outside the present Negro neighborhoods," Davis wrote.

When the couple moved in, there were petitions spread that protested them living among the white residents of the community. Some of the talk suggested violent action, according to an NAACP letter obtained from the Library of Congress.

Racism pervaded the community from 1923 until the 1960s. Blackface minstrel shows were still in vogue in Johnstown and were performed in local churches and among civic groups. They were discontinued when black activist groups protested them.

The 1960s were particularly challenging but also a landmark decade of accomplishment and leadership for the local NAACP.

The more violent white people were toward people in the civil rights movement, the more tested those within the movement were. Some wanted a more confrontational tack taken with the racists they were protesting. Others pointed to the progress they had made with the nonviolent approach, arguing it should be continued. The Johnstown NAACP took a stance as the national movement was splintering between those who wanted to continue in the tradition of nonviolent protest and those who wanted a more militant mentality. Leaders in the city's branch disavowed the Black Power movement, as the latter philosophy was known.

"The local branch does not condone, advocate or support this type of action, nor does the branch recognize or adhere to the philosophy underlying this action," the executive board said in a letter to the *Tribune-Democrat* of Johnstown in 1966. "We realize that there are causes for this type of action. However, we feel that this is not the way to solve the problem."

The assassination of Martin Luther King Jr. in April 1968 tested the local black community and African Americans across the country. While race riots happened elsewhere, Johnstown managed to maintain the peace with the help of some older adults in the local NAACP. They patrolled the streets to make sure black youths didn't commit crime.

Later, in 1968, the local branch sponsored a Black Heritage Festival at the Cambria County War Memorial. The idea was to give both black and white people in Greater Johnstown an opportunity to see the accomplishments, talents, strengths and overall contributions made by African Americans, according to an article that ran in the *Johnstown Observer*. The event featured outstanding individuals in entertainment, sports, arts and science.

"At the present time many knowledgeable people consider racism—white and black combined—as posing a greater threat than communism to the security, progress and general welfare of our country," leaders within the organization told the *Observer*. "This is ironic, to say the least, in a nation that was founded by persons, many of whom left their native land to escape discrimination, intolerance and suppression—things which have been major factors in the growth of racism."

In cities throughout America, stories of police brutality and the premature deaths of black youths are a troubling part of history. Johnstown is no different. In 1969, Charles LaPorta Jr., a Johnstown police officer, shot fifteen-year-old African American Tim Perkins. The shooting brought outrage and once again tested the leadership of black clergymen and members of the NAACP. They rose to the challenge, particularly the Reverend W.M. Cunningham, pastor of First Cambria A.M.E. Zion Church.

"The issues raised by both blacks and whites and by me are the standards set by our police department," Cunningham released in a statement to the *Tribune-Democrat*. "Are churchgoers, teenagers en route to home, hospitals or dances to be pounced upon and labeled purse-snatchers, loudmouth bullies, troublemakers and so forth, solely because they are assembled or are traveling on the street?"

The last few decades have brought the challenges of rising unemployment and underemployment. As industry and steel mills left the city, the jobless rate in the African American community rose. Education is something the NAACP now emphasizes, according to Alan Cashaw, the current president of the organization.

"If you get educated, and you let it lead the way, you'll find access to jobs and housing," Cashaw said. "You'll have access to voting because you know what your rights are. And you'll stay out of the criminal justice system."

The Johnstown NAACP pushes for diversity clubs in local high schools. Cashaw said the hope of the local NAACP is to instill an appreciation for black culture among white youths. The hope is that such encounters will lead to a more tolerant philosophy among the local population.

"We think over the next fifty years, the culture will be diverse and embracing," Cashaw said. "Instead of right now, when you know someone's different, you don't associate or know anything about them. We think a lot of our efforts are mitigated by what is taught at home. Parents at home have to encourage children to mix with people and get to know them. They don't have to necessarily have them as their best friend. When we get to that point, our race relations will have come a long way."

Black citizens of Johnstown have also, for most of the city's history, not been able to exercise the full potential of their right to vote because there is little precinct voting. Most elections are at-large and were determined by white voters. There have been a few African American city managers, and recently the public voted in its first two black city council members.

White supremacist beliefs still prevail in many of the communities near Johnstown. It's not uncommon to see Confederate flags hanging outside homes in the countryside. In 1992, a branch of the Ku Klux Klan was founded in Johnstown again. There is a white militia in the Laurel Highlands, where Johnstown is located, that was in Charlottesville, Virginia, when that rally was held in 2017. They are actively recruiting members. And most recently, in late 2018, members of the Ku Klux Klan dropped recruiting materials on people's driveways in nearby communities telling of the danger of integration and mixing with Jewish and black people. The letters, which were weighed down in plastic bags by popcorn seeds, trafficked in the same old stereotypes. Black men were dangerous to white women and to each other, far more so than the Ku Klux Klan ever was, according to the organization.

Samuel W. Black, of the Heinz History Center, said he doesn't try to rate racism as lesser or greater. But he said because there are larger black

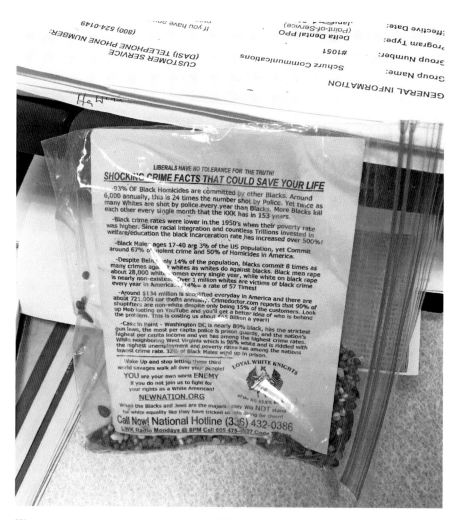

Klan recruiters passed out material in late 2018 as part of a statewide effort to increase membership. They trafficked in many of the old stereotypes to do so, including using misleading statistics without any attribution that argued black men were more likely to rape white women. *Photo by the author.*

populations in Pittsburgh, Philadelphia, Erie and Harrisburg, that sometimes those cities may be more welcoming than the parts of the state that lie in between. African Americans find refuge in urban areas, he said.

"Because those areas have not always been welcoming to people of color and there's a history there," Black said. "I completely understand that history, and it's not a new phenomenon to me. It's really hard to say though that this area was worse than that area. Bad is bad."

What Johnstown lost because of the order is unclear. Many of those who left, or their children or grandchildren, could have started businesses, become political leaders and established themselves as productive members of society. Cauffiel set the city back decades. There would have been more black-owned businesses and more African American leaders. It's a human disaster that is on level with the three great floods. And it's a catastrophe that should be remembered to understand the current state of the city. As one woman said to the *Tribune-Democrat*, "Rosedale was never the same."

Johnstown became a less attractive place for black people who wanted to come to the North in the ensuing decades. From 1923 to the 1930 census, the African American population dropped from an estimated 3,000 to 1,444, reversing the trend of growth that had been seen the decade before, when it nearly quadrupled.

As Loewen made the case in his book, communities that excluded people on the basis of race or other identifiers historically have stifled economic growth and innovation. When driving through Johnstown today, the largest impression left is the largely underused steel mill that is a remnant from its past. Whether or not Johnstown could have weathered the steel mill closing with a more diverse economy is a matter of conjecture. But the racial cleansing and historical marginalization of minorities there didn't attract entrepreneurs at the same rate as Pittsburgh.

"For the rural sundown town, it makes them backward," Loewen said. "Usually people are shy about bringing in new industry because they bring in different people. A lot of these places become economically backward."

The neighborhood gradually disappeared from the city's landscape. People remembered Rosedale as a black neighborhood, but many forgot what happened in 1923. But nonetheless, those who drove by it had a sense that something historically important happened there. Bob Sargeant, a local resident, used to turn off Benshoff Hill Road near the top of a hill and head toward Johnstown in the 1960s. It was rough for a car. But he was on an ATV. The road was old and abandoned. Once away from Benshoff, there was a small town of old abandoned single-family homes and small buildings, all cheaply constructed of plywood, like World War II instant barracks. It looked like the whole place was abandoned at once, he remembered. He didn't know that it was Rosedale until later.

"The place was really eerie. The houses were very poorly built, not like 'company houses' built by mining companies," Sargeant said. "It was a long time ago, but the place was just sad. There were little picket fences, swing sets, maybe…little flourishes to make it nice and like a community, and it just looked like everyone just took off. It was so spooky that I thought I would be violating something if I got off the bike. I thought maybe it had something to do with an emergency man-up for the war."

In a survey conducted in the 1940s among African Americans, Florence Hornback, a scholar who studied the community during that time, concluded that the problems besetting the black community were not exclusively their own. They troubled all of Johnstown.

"The problems of the colored population are not confined to that group but represent the problems of the entire community," Hornback wrote. "A city or a borough which is allowed to deteriorate soon loses its attraction for those who wish to live in an environment that is conducive to good health and happy living, and the community finds itself with a dwindling population because, in such a tightly knit urban area, the conditions which prevail in any section affect the whole.

"Readily distinguishable because of color, the Negro is a convenient object for prejudice," she continued.[62]

This banishment was seldom talked about in the decades that followed. It wasn't passed down to later generations. When speaking to someone from Johnstown, especially a white person, most don't know it happened. It was not something that their parents discussed. Elliot Jaspin, author of *Buried in Bitter Waters: The Hidden History of Racial Cleansing in America*, studied the phenomenon in his book. Jaspin explained why racial cleansings, or expulsions as they are sometimes known, have been forgotten or not accounted for in textbooks and by local historians.

"Obviously for whites, this is a difficult history," Jaspin said. "Since it occurred so long ago, my best guess is there is no one alive today that saw this happen. But it's our grandparents and great-grandparents that were engaged in this as whites. Thinking that grandpa took part in a racial cleansing is not something that fills you up with pride. So you create a fable to deal with the fact that this event took place or to dissociate or even deny it and move on from there. It's not something you want to own."

Jaspin said it is difficult to find black people to discuss racial cleansings.

"My guess is it was something parents didn't want to tell children," Jaspin said. "In terms of an oral history, it's been pretty much lost. I can't recall finding any contemporaneous accounts in someone writing a letter to someone else. In the black community, that was very rare."

If knowing this story does anything, hopefully it will cause people to seek justice for those who were affected by it. It's not merely an ancient story that has no impact on people today. This event happened in 1923, which means it's well within the range for potential lawsuits for the heirs of those who were affected by the systematic and institutional expulsion of two entire races from a city in violation of their constitutionally mandated rights. Reparations should be a topic of discussion when addressing this part of local and state history and the need to prevent it from happening again. And Johnstown isn't the only community in which lawsuits could happen. Loewen estimates that the number of Pennsylvania sundown towns and communities, where there were efforts to keep out or expel black people, could hover around seven hundred.

"Reparations scares the pants off white folks," Loewen said. "First, get them to admit they were a sundown town. Second, apologize and then say they were wrong. Then third, they should say we were wrong and sorry and we don't do it anymore. And the third one has to have teeth. That can be reparations."

Marco Williams suggested that cities guilty of these crimes should at the very least erect a monument acknowledging it happened. Johnstown doesn't have that at this point insofar as the 1923 incident is concerned.

Part of Johnstown's redemption must include an effort to embrace people of varying backgrounds—including those who differ in race, religion, sexual orientation and gender identity. A national initiative called All-In Cities has called upon local leaders who are ready to do so. Johnstown should join with other cities in pushing that agenda. Forming new models of equitable growth and development requires transforming policies and systems that have perpetuated racial inequities. For a city that has struggled to reinvent itself economically, the first step may be celebrating diversity as it tries to create new industries. Innovation comes from different viewpoints, often those held by minorities.

The hope of the people who remained in Johnstown following Cauffiel's order was much like other people of color across the country. Distrust of white people was an issue for decades following the order. But many black people preached faith in their fellow man.

"We try to level with our children," one-time Johnstown NAACP president James Porcher told the *Tribune-Democrat* in 1980. "I teach my children that not every black man is a friend and not every white man is an enemy. We have to judge each person by his actions."[63]

AFTERWORD

This project has been five years in the making. Johnstown is steeped in history, but it is mostly famous for the great Johnstown Flood of 1889, about which David McCullough wrote brilliantly. Richard Burkert, president of the Johnstown Area Heritage Association, mentioned this injustice to me when I wanted to do a black history story.

In using current research methods, including online newspaper databases, I was able to see that it was a national scandal. And so began the research for a newspaper series that later appeared in the *Somerset Daily American*, a publication I have the pleasure of working for. The initial reaction from our readers, white and black, was "I can't believe this happened. I never heard of it before."

Upon the suggestion of my editor Brian Whipkey and colleague Tom Koppenhofer, I decided to turn the newspaper series into a book. And the research led me to Washington, D.C., to the Library of Congress, the state archives in Harrisburg and various libraries throughout western Pennsylvania. It also served as the impetus for the Rosedale Oral History Project, which has thousands of supporters on Facebook. The aim of the project is to track down the descendants of people who were forced out of any community on the basis of race, religion or identity. The transcripts of those interviews, and all the research done for this book, will be turned over to a local museum.

The tendency to vilify entire races, religions and minorities because of the actions of one or a few of its members still exists. It sometimes still serves as a governing philosophy for people of all levels of and positions in government. It's an easier way of looking at things and an easier thing to portray to the public when the candidates canvass for votes. It still appeals to some voters in the greater Johnstown area and places like it. One can hope that people who undertake such a strategy will experience the same electoral fate as Joseph Cauffiel.

At the very least, they will be remembered as the disgraceful figures they are, much like Cauffiel is. His defining legacy is what he did to the people of Rosedale and surrounding black neighborhoods. And thus goes the warning to current and future politicians contemplating such a method and strategy. You will be remembered for it. And you won't be remembered well.

Much like newspapers in Johnstown told people to be wary of their prejudices for fear of being exploited by a political leader, people in America today should be just as keen of their own prejudices for the same reason. Enabling those people, who will continue to play to their worst instincts, can often lead to terrible injustices and atrocities. And the people who empower the perpetrators are complicit.

Most of the injustices we see carried out today have historical precedent. By studying them, we see how people dealt with it in previous instances. And we see the things that were effective in combating them.

ACKNOWLEDGEMENTS

This book wouldn't have been possible without the support and efforts of numerous people. First and foremost, I want to thank my editor Brian Whipkey and general manager Becky Flyte, who gave me the time to work on this for my newspaper. I count myself as fortunate to write about something this weighty so early in my career. It is remarkable for a newspaper with limited resources to dedicate the money and labor to document an instance of terrible injustice that happened nearly a century ago.

Secondly, the editors involved in this book improved it and gave it structure, vision and coherence. My father, Jerry McDevitt, ripped this apart with as much scrutiny as he gives the young associates in his law firm. As a result, the book got a recommended structure that took me nearly a year to accomplish. He has been a rock in my life and is always there to encourage me and keep me grounded. The second editor, Eric Boyd, told me to include contemporary perspectives, which gave the book a dimension that it didn't have when it was a straight narrative. The third editor, Brian Schrock, edited the copy to make sure the sentences flowed well and read easily. Without all three, the text of the book wouldn't have been at the quality it is today. And I can't express enough gratitude for the editorial guidance provided by Elliot Jaspin. Having a Pulitzer Prize winner take the time to offer insights on where my manuscript could improve was priceless as a learning experience.

I'd like to thank Alisha Wormsley and Tony Norman for doing the cover and writing the foreword. For them to lend their name to this project gave it a credibility that I wouldn't have had if they hadn't been involved. The same could be said for the numerous authors, journalists, historians and professors who offered their insights for the book. They made points that I wouldn't have and that illuminated this part of history.

I'd like to thank Doug Heuck at *Pittsburgh Quarterly* for publishing a version of this story in his magazine. Doug has been a mentor to me in the past few years and has offered guidance to me both professionally and personally. There's a reason why he wins so many awards at the Golden Quills.

As I DID WITH my first book, I'd like to thank my close friends George Janusz and Jeremy Norman, with whom I shared developments of this project. They have been among my closest buddies for the last few years. My family was also likewise supportive. I wouldn't be where I am today without Hilary, Kelly, A.J., Sabrina, Casey, Kristine, mom, Lori, Jack, Josie and Josh. In life, you have to cherish and value those who offer unconditional love and support.

I'd like to thank my publisher, The History Press, for continuing to give me an opportunity to release books and Banks Smither in particular for offering me my second book deal. I've been fortunate to publish two compositions that became important documents of local history. It is my hope to continue to do so.

Anyone or any publication, including the *Pittsburgh Courier*, that has highlighted this work and project has helped advance it. So my gratitude extends to them as well.

One of the things that I've learned throughout all of this is to continue to defend and speak out in support of your deeply held convictions. While others may doubt your motives, in your heart and mind you know what you want to stand for. Have faith that your work and life will carry out those principles.

NOTES

Shock and the Search for a Cause

1. Special section on "Black History," *Johnstown Tribune-Democrat*, February 12, 1980.
2. Ibid.
3. Ibid.
4. Sherman, "Johnstown v. the Negro," 454–64.
5. Special section on "Black History."
6. Arnesen, *Black Protest and the Great Migration.*
7. "Importation of Negroes Opposed," *Johnstown Tribune*, August 2, 1919.
8. Brody, *Steelworkers in America.*
9. English, Report of John N. English to the Attorney General of Pennsylvania, Gifford Pinchot Papers, box 1499, Manuscripts Division, Library of Congress.
10. Dickerson, *Out of the Crucible.*
11. Hollis and Hollis, *Saga of the Johnstown City Schools.*

Bad Elements and Bad Reactions

12. "Police Officials Not Anticipating Any Disturbance," *Johnstown Tribune*, August 6, 1917.
13. "City Takes Steps to Stop Possible Race Riots Here," *Johnstown Tribune*, July 31, 1917.

14. "Franklin Borough Is Said to Be Mecca for 'Bad' Negroes," *Johnstown Tribune*, September 12, 1920.
15. "No Change Reported as Officers Grimly Battle in Hospitals," *Johnstown Tribune*, September 1, 1923.
16. "Mayor Visits Hill District," *Johnstown Tribune*, March 4, 1919.
17. "Wave of Crime on 'The Hill,'" *Johnstown Tribune*, February 24, 1919.
18. "Declares There Was a 'Frame-up' to Get Her," *Johnstown Tribune*, August 2, 1918.
19. "More Police for Outlying Sections," *Johnstown Tribune*, February 13, 1919.
20. "Wage Increase for the Policemen Impossible Now, Is the Decision," *Johnstown Tribune*, July 11, 1918.
21. "Officer Shot to Save Self," *Johnstown Tribune*, December 4, 1918; "Policeman Kills Negro Following Fight at Franklin," *Johnstown Tribune*, December 3, 1918.
22. "Negro Slays Wife with Ax," *Johnstown Tribune*, May 22, 1920.
23. Craig, *Ku Klux Klan in Western Pennsylvania*; Loucks, *Ku Klux Klan in Pennsylvania*.
24. "A Ku Klux Klan Branch for Indiana," *Indiana Weekly Messenger*, March 9, 1992.

The Spark

25. *Somerset Herald*, "Negro Settlement Closely Guarded." September 1, 1923.
26. English, Report.
27. "Memorial Places Conveniences at Officers' Demand," *Johnstown Tribune*, September 1, 1923.

Fever Heat

28. "No Change Reported as Officers Grimly Battle in Hospitals," *Johnstown Tribune*, September 1, 1923.
29. Ibid.
30. "Death of County Detective Holds Up Prosecutions," *Johnstown Tribune*, September 1, 1923.
31. "No Change Reported."
32. "Memorial Places Conveniences."

The Overlord

33. "Joseph Cauffiel Named Defendant in Suit Recorded," *Johnstown Tribune*, July 26, 1917.
34. "Mayor Tells Man He Needs Beating Instead of Fine," *Johnstown Tribune*, October 4, 1920.
35. "Mayor Uses Police Power to Close Up Bars of Defendants," *Johnstown Tribune*, December 29, 1920.
36. "Selling Whiskey Is Same as Bartering in Humans—Mayor," *Johnstown Tribune*, December 16, 1920.

Keeping the Peace

37. "Police Officers Improve Slightly, Reports Indicate," *Johnstown Tribune*, September 3, 1923.
38. Ibid.
39. "Rosedale," *Johnstown Tribune*, September 1, 1923.

The Order

40. English, Report.
41. "Mayor Cauffiel Says Undesirable Negroes Must Quit Johnstown," *Johnstown Democrat*, September 7, 1923.

Burning Intolerance

42. "Benefit Festival Monday Night for Policemen Relief," *Johnstown Tribune*, September 15, 1923; "Benefit Affairs Planned to Help Fund for Police," *Johnstown Tribune*, September 15, 1923; "Benefit Will Be Held Tonight for Policemen's Fund," *Johnstown Tribune*, September 17, 1923; "More than $1,300 Added to Officers' Fund from Circus," *Johnstown Tribune*, September 20, 1923.
43. "City Officials Call on Wounded Officers," *Johnstown Tribune*, September 6, 1923.
44. "Detective Otto Nukem Succumbs of Heart Attack," *Johnstown Tribune*, September 13, 1923.

Taking Notice

45. Bunie, *Robert L. Vann of the Pittsburgh Courier*.

National Furor

46. Sullivan, *Lift Every Voice*.

The Governor

47. Reels 31 and 33, in American Civil Liberties Union Archives, the Roger Baldwin Years 1917–1950, Manuscript Division, Library of Congress.
48. Walker, *In Defense of American Liberties*.

Repudiation

49. "The Primaries," *Johnstown Tribune*, September 17, 1923.
50. "Spectacular Contests Mark Primary Election in City," *Johnstown Tribune*, September 19, 1923.
51. "Undesirable Publicity," *Johnstown Tribune*, September 22, 1923.
52. Whittle, *Johnstown, Pennsylvania, Part 1*.

Growing Outrage

53. "Mayor Will Drive Negroes from City," *Monroe Journal*, September 18, 1923.

Southern Propaganda

54. Letter from J.S. Wannamaker to Gifford Pinchot, in Gifford Pinchot Papers, box 1499, Manuscript Division, Library of Congress.
55 Michaeli, *Defender*.

State Investigation

56. Wilson, *Selected Writings of James Weldon Johnson.*
57. English, Report.

Aftermath

58. Garvey, *Philosophy and Opinions of Marcus Garvey.*
59. McDevitt, "Oldest Black Church in Johnstown Led the Way on Civil Rights."
60. Arneson, *Black Protest and the Great Migration.*
61. Owens, "Johnstown Trouble Laid to 'Set-Up' Negro."
62. Hornback, *Survey of the Negro Population.*
63. Special section on "Black History."

BIBLIOGRAPHY

Akron (OH) Beacon Journal. "A Hometown Dictator Falls." October 3, 1923.

Alexander City (AL) Outlook. "Negroes in Johnston." September 26, 1923.

———. "Northern Outrages against Negroes." September 26, 1923.

Altoona (PA) Mirror. "Two Officers Are Killed in Battle." August 31, 1923.

Altoona (PA) Times. "Threats of Lynching Are Made in Patton." September 27, 1904.

Altoona (PA) Tribune. "Cauffiel 'Advised' Negroes to Depart." September 20, 1923.

———. "Drunk Negro Uses Razor on Another." June 25, 1918.

———. "In Other Counties." October 16, 1909.

———. "Johnstown's Shame." September 19, 1923.

———. "Justified." September 24, 1923.

———. "Mayor's Court Plan Attracts Attention." December 21, 1923.

———. "Negroes Ordered from Johnstown." September 10, 1923.

———. "Negro Gunman Arrested Here." May 15, 1922.

———. "Negro Welfare Leader Makes Address Here." October 19, 1923.

———. "Southern Negroes, Out of Employment, Travel Back to the Home Land." November 21, 1923.

———. "Terms Johnstown Incident Disgrace to Pennsylvania." September 26, 1923.

Anniston (AL) Star. "Johnstown's Mayor and the Way He Does Things." September 22, 1923.

Argus Leader (Sioux Falls, SD). "An Audacious Mayor." September 26, 1923.

———. "Angry Mob Raged." January 31, 1907.

Arnesen, Eric. *Black Protest and the Great Migration: A Brief History with Documents.* Boston: Bedford/St. Martin's, 2003.

Asheville (NC) Citizen-Times. "The Race Problem in Spruce Pine." September 29, 1923.

Austin (TX) American. "On the Road Again." September 27, 1923.

Baltimore (MD) Sun. "Cotton Men Take Up Negro's Cause." September 23, 1923.

———. "Johnstown Trouble Laid to 'Set-Up' Negro." September 27, 1923.

———. "State Starts Investigation." September 23, 1923.

Bane, Ralph. Letter from Ralph Bane to Gifford Pinchot. From Gifford Pinchot Papers, Box 1499, Manuscripts Division, Library of Congress.

Berger, Karl. *Johnstown: The Story of a Unique Valley.* Johnstown, PA: Johnstown Flood Museum, 1985.

Borton, Walter. Letter from Walter Borton to Gifford Pinchot. From Gifford Pinchot Papers, Box 1499, Manuscripts Division, Library of Congress.

Bradford (PA) Era. "Would Protect the Colored Residents." September 19, 1923.

Brody, David. *Steelworkers in America: The Nonunion Era.* Chicago: University of Illinois Press, 1998.

Buffalo (NY) American. "Governor Acts Promptly in Deportation." September 27, 1923.

———. "The N.A.A.C.P." October 11, 1923.

Bunie, Andrew. *Robert L. Vann of the Pittsburgh Courier: Politics and Black Journalism.* Pittsburgh: University of Pittsburgh Press, 1974.

Capper's Weekly (Topeka, KS). "Persons Guilty of Crimes." September 29, 1923.

Chamber of Council Minutes, October 23, 1923, Pennsylvania State Archives, Roll 5506.

Chamber of Council Minutes, September 11, 1923, Pennsylvania State Archives, Roll 5505.

Chicago Defender. "Getting Rough." September 22, 1923.

———. "Mexican Government Investigates Johnstown Exodus." September 29, 1923.

———. "When a Protest Counts." September 29, 1923.

———. "You Will Do Well." September 22, 1923.

Cincinnati (OH) Enquirer. "'Negroes Must Pack and Go,' Johnstown Mayor Declares; Governor Rules Otherwise." September 19, 1923.

———. "Negroes Told to Leave Town." September 15, 1923.

Clarke County Democrat (Grove Hill, AL). "The Negro in the North." October 18, 1923.

Clayton (AL) Record. "Mistreating Our Southern Negroes." October 5, 1923.

Cleveland (OH) Star. "Johnstown Mayor Orders Negroes Leave." September 18, 1923.

———. "Mayor Declares All Negroes Must Go." September 28, 1923.

Collier, B.G. Letter from B.G. Collier to Gifford Pinchot. From Gifford Pinchot Papers, Box 1499, Manuscripts Division, Library of Congress.

Coppin, L.J. Letter from L.J. Coppin, J.H. Smith and Geo. A Brown to Gifford Pinchot. From Gifford Pinchot Papers, Box 1499, Manuscripts Division, Library of Congress.

Courier-Journal. "Negroes at the North." September 15, 1923.

Craig, John. *The Ku Klux Klan in Western Pennsylvania, 1921–1928.* Bethlehem, PA: Lehigh University Press. 2015.

Daily Deadwood (SD) Pioneer-Times. "Official Law-Breaking." September 28, 1923.

Daily News. "Johnstown Mayor Orders Negroes to Get Out of City." September 10, 1923.

Daily Republican. "National Guard May Be Called." September 29, 1904.

Daily Times. "The Negro Problem in the North." September 27, 1923.

Detroit (MI) Free Press. "Baptist Preacher Expires Suddenly." June 15, 1928.

———. "The End of a Career." October 10, 1923.

Dickerson, Dennis C. *Out of the Crucible: Black Steelworkers in Western Pennsylvania.* Albany: State University of New York Press, 1986.

Douglas, Davison. *Jim Crow Moves North: The Battle over Northern School Segregation, 1865–1954.* New York: Cambridge University Press, 2005.

El Informador (Jalisco, MX). "Parece Que Termino el Incidente de Johnston, Penn." September 23, 1923.

English. John. Report of John N. English to the Attorney General of Pennsylvania. From Gifford Pinchot Papers, Box 1499, Manuscripts Division, Library of Congress.

Enterprise-Tocsin (Indianola, MS). "Daylight Dawning." September 27, 1923.

Evening News. "Cauffiel Is Still on War Path Against Own Party." October 10, 1924.

———. "Johnstown Is Stirred by Negro Church." October 6, 1923.

———. "Negroes Never Were Ordered to Quit Johnstown." October 4, 1923.

———. "Pinchot Has Two Ways of Protecting Rights of Johnstown Negroes." September 24, 1923.

———. "Pinchot Orders Investigation." September 22, 1923.

———. "Pinchot Orders Johnstown Case to Be Investigated." September 22, 1923.

———. "Pinchot Says He Will Safeguard…" September 19, 1923.

———. "State Labor Demand Shows a Decrease." July 10, 1923.

Evening Report. "Reaping the Whirlwind." September 29, 1923.

Evening Standard. "Current Comment." September 24, 1923.

Evening Sun. "Johnstown Bars Southern Negroes." September 15, 1923.

Fort Wayne (IN) Journal-Gazette. "Is the Boll Weevil Changing the Black Belt?" September 30, 1923.

———. "The Mayor of Johnstown." September 21, 1923.

Fulton Democrat (Canton, IL). "Plans Survey of Social Work." November 8, 1923.

Gaffney (SC) Ledger. "The Pot and the Kettle." September 20, 1923.

Garvey, Marcus. *Philosophy and Opinions of Marcus Garvey.* New York: Brawtley Press, 2014.

———. *Selected Writings and Speeches of Marcus Garvey.* Mineola, NY: Dover Publications, 2004.

Gazzam, Mrs. Joseph. Letter from Mrs. Joseph Gazzam to Gifford Pinchot. From Gifford Pinchot Papers, Box 1499, Manuscripts Division, Library of Congress.

Gettysburg (PA) Times. "City's Mayor Is Still Defiant." September 19, 1923.

Gordon, Linda. *The Second Coming of the KKK: The Ku Klux Klan of the 1920s and the American Political Tradition.* New York: Liverwright Publishing Corporation, 2017.

Graves, Joseph. Letter from Joseph Graves to Gifford Pinchot. From Gifford Pinchot Papers, Box 1499, Manuscripts Division, Library of Congress.

Great Falls (MT) Tribune. "The Power of a City Executive." September 24, 1923.

Griffith, Randy. "Wilmore, Laurel Hill among Early Settlements." *Johnstown Tribune-Democrat*, February 28, 2010.

Hamilton (OH) Evening Journal. "Ditching the Constitution." October 5, 1923.

Hardy, Elias. Letter from Elias Hardy to Gifford Pinchot. From Gifford Pinchot Papers, Box 1499, Manuscripts Division, Library of Congress.

Harris, J. Silas. Letter from J. Silas Harris to Gifford Pinchot. From Gifford Pinchot Papers, Box 1499, Manuscripts Division, Library of Congress.

Harrisburg (PA) Telegraph. "Call It a Day." September 8, 1923.

———. "Cauffiel Takes Middle Course in Exile Order." September 20, 1923.

———. "Johnstown Mayor Makes Poor Showing." September 19, 1923.

————. "The Negro's Progress." August 20, 1923.

Hinkson, Haven. Letter from Haven Hinkson to Gifford Pinchot. From Gifford Pinchot Papers, Box 1499, Manuscripts Division, Library of Congress.

Hollis, Clea, and Leah Hollis. *The Saga of the Johnstown City Schools*. Johnstown, PA: Patliss Press, 2003.

Holloway, Roscoe. "'Get Out,' Mayor to Citizens." *Chicago Defender*, September 22, 1923.

Hornback, Florence Mary. *Survey of the Negro Population of Metropolitan Johnstown, Pennsylvania*. Johnstown, PA: Johnstown Tribune and Democrat, 1941.

Houston (TX) Post. "The 'Migration' About Ended." September 20, 1923.

Huntingdon Press. "Mexico Asks Quiz of Mayor's Edict." September 20, 1923.

Huntington Press. "Black Belt Stays in Dixie; Negroes Leave North." September 30, 1923.

————. "Johnstown Mayor Insists No Formal Order." September 20, 1923.

————. "Mexico Asks Quiz of Mayor's Edict." September 20, 1923.

Hutchinson (KS) News. "Two Thousand Negroes Left." July 14, 2016.

Indiana Gazette. "Crazed Negro Kills 2 Officers and Wounds 3." August 31, 1923.

————. "Johnstown Mayor Orders Negroes 'Out.'" September 7, 1923.

————. "Ku Klux Klan Branch to Be Formed Here." March 1, 1922.

————. "Negroes Heed Mayor's Order." September 8, 1923.

————. "State Probe in Johnstown Ends." September 25, 1923.

Indianapolis (IN) Star. "Negro Residents of Johnstown, Pa., Driven from City." September 15, 1923.

Indiana Weekly Messenger. "A Ku Klux Branch for Indiana." March 9, 1922.

————. "Newsy Paragraphs." September 13, 1923.

Iola (KS) Daily Register and Evening News. "It Appears Now that the Mayor." September 21, 1923.

————. "Orders Negroes to Quit Town." July 14, 2016.

Ithaca (NY) Journal. "Coolidge Sees Delegation of Colored Women." September 20, 1923.

————. "Johnstown's Ku Klux Mayor." September 21, 1923.

————. "Official Lawlessness Costly." April 17, 1924.

Jaspin, Elliot. *Buried in Bitter Waters: The Hidden History of Racial Cleansing in America*. New York: Basic Books, 2008.

Johnson, James W. Letter from James Weldon Johnson to Gifford Pinchot. From Gifford Pinchot Papers, Box 1499, Manuscripts Division, Library of Congress.

———. Telegram from James Weldon Johnson to Gifford Pinchot. From Gifford Pinchot Papers, Box 1499, Manuscripts Division, Library of Congress.

Johnstown City Charter, Pennsylvania Room, Cambria County Library.

Johnstown (PA) Democrat. "American Legion Minstrel Show 'Going Over' Big." May 31, 1922.

———. "Argument in Cauffiel Cases Set for April 19." April 9, 1921.

———. "Believe Bender and Grachan Have Good Chance." September 3, 1923.

———. "Chief Briney Attended Birthday Party January of Last Year." February 17, 1922.

———. "Close Race for Mayor Between Cauffiel and Stockton." November 9, 1927.

———. "Colonization of Negroes in This Vicinity." November 21, 1916.

———. "Colored Woman Not Able to Tell How She Was Shot." December 5, 1921.

———. "Congressman Warren Worth Bailey Tells Audience that the Election Showed Need of Economic Education." November 15, 1916.

———. "County Detective John A. James and Detective Joseph Abrahams Are Slain." August 31, 1923.

———. "Cruelly Battered Body of Seven-Year-Old Found in Cellar." October 27, 1921.

———. "Democrat to Construct a Seven Story Building for Newspaper Plant." March 10, 1919.

———. "Dem Sunday Rules Slap at Alien Rivals." January 15, 1920.

———. "Detective Otto Nukem Dies of Heart Failure." September 14, 1923.

———. "Dr. Kinkaid Makes Reply to Dr. Barnes' Lecture Regards to Race." April 7, 1921.

———. "Fonesca, Mexican, Is Simply Refusing to Be Registered for War." June 13, 1917.

———. "Governor Starts Investigation of Cauffiel's Order." September 19, 1923.

———. "How Did He Do It" November 12, 1927.

———. "Impounding of Ballot Boxes in City Is Rumored." November 29, 1927.

———. "Joseph Cauffiel." July 11, 1932.

———. "Joseph Cauffiel, Three Times Mayor, Succumbs to Prolonged Illness." July 11, 1932.

———. "Kirby Is Acquitted of Assault on Negro." March 9, 1920.

———. "Ku Klux Klan Members Hear Sensational Discussion by Grand Dragon on Its Policies." November 11, 1927.

———. "Ku Klux Klan Reported to Have Broadened Out." March 15, 1922.

———. "Many New Combinations Enter to Change Political Aspects." October 29, 1920.

———. "Mayor Cauffiel Declares He Is, 'Cleaning Up the City.'" January 19, 1922.

———. "Mayor Cauffiel Not the Only One Who Wore Overalls." May 4, 1920.

———. "Mayor Cauffiel Says Toy Gun Was Pointed at George Wright." April 6, 1921.

———. "Mayor Cauffiel Says Undesirable Negroes Must Quit Johnstown." September 7, 1923.

———. "Mayor Joe Probably Will Go after Renomination." August 8, 1923.

———. "Mayor Suspends Chief Briney." February 14, 1922.

———. "Method of Tallying Split Party Tickets Reported to Have Been Changed by Computation Board." November 22, 1927.

———. "Mixing the Labor Problem," *Johnstown Democrat*, December 6, 1919.

———. "A Modern Instance." February 15, 1922.

———. "Murder Charge Against Colored Man Brought Here." May 13, 1922.

———. "Negro Charged with Shooting Affray Is Jailed." May 14, 1922.

———. "Negroes Brought from Alabama Arrested for Sending Liquor by Mail." November 21, 1916.

———. "Negroes Leaving by Hundreds and More Are Ready." September 8, 1923.

———. "Negro Slasher Is Arrested." October 14, 1923.

———. "Negro Slayer Says His Name Is Davis; Admits Other Crimes in South." April 12, 1922.

———. "Negro Suspected of Murder Is Reported as Being Under Arrest." November 5, 1921.

———. "Negro Witnesses Say Self-Defense Caused a Killing." December 16, 1921.

———. "Nineteen Are Taken in Raid." March 10, 1920.

———. "No Motive Other than Quarrel yet Developed in Slaying of Colored Workman by Another." April 11, 1922.

———. "No Serious Shortage of Work Here, Claims Employment Official." March 13, 1919.

———. "Officer Shot to Save Self." December 4, 1918.

———. "Part of the Fullness of a Full Heart." May 25, 1922.

———. "Police Silent after Session with Negro." February 21, 1920.

———. "Prosecutor Claims Mayor Cauffiel Asked to Bring Suit..." March 14, 1922.

———. "Rosedale Negro Suspect Is Missing." October 29, 1921.

———. "Scarcity of Labor Shown in the Report of..." February 20, 1920.

———. "'Seething Volcano' Story Is Resented by All Interest." February 16, 1919.

———. "Threats Heard during Day County." September 11, 1923.

———. "The Tragedy at Rosedale." September 11, 1923.

———. "Tribune Occupies New Home..." October 18, 1920.

———. "Tribune's Managing Editor Has Exciting Encounter with Mayor at City Hall." February 21, 1922.

———. "Twelve Crosses Burned by Ku Klux Klan Here." September 8, 1923.

———. "Two Roses too Many for Walters." February 19, 1920.

———. "Wants Clergyman to Be the Chief of Police." December 17, 1911.

———. "Was Delegate to Paris Conference." December 6, 1919.

———. "Wave of Crime Seems to Be Sweeping City; Negro Is Under Arrest." February 16, 1919.

———. "Worse than Darkest Africa." May 17, 1922.

Johnstown (PA) Tribune. "Aged Mexican Was Beaten and Robbed." April 19, 1918.

———. "Alleged Murderer of Negro Laborer Makes Complete Confession." April 11, 1922.

———. "Alleged Negro Is Thief Who Looted Many Hen Houses." April 15, 1922.

———. "Alleged Slayer Captured While Hiding in Shack." February 8, 1919.

———. "Alleged Slayer of Alabama Man Held by Police." May 13, 1922.

———. "Amusement Park Is Being Planned." July 6, 1922.

———. "Ancient Scheme Went Wrong Way." August 23, 1918.

———. "Angry Mob Awaits Negro at Patton." September 22, 1904.

———. "Assess Big Fine on Negro Driver in Auto Smash." May 6, 1921.

———. "Bailey Slanders Women Who Are Helping Make Path Easy for Voters." October 29, 1920.

———. "Baltimore Negro Is Identified in Hennecamp Death." May 26, 1921.

———. "Barber William Banks Now in His 60th Year." January 29, 1919.

———. "Benefit Affairs Planned to Help Fund for Police." September 15, 1923.

———. "Benefit Festival Monday Night for Policemen Relief." September 15, 1923.

———. "Benefit Will Be Held Tonight for Policemen's Fund." September 17, 1923.

———. "Bolivar Officers Get Negro Fugitive After He Broke From Lockup." October 14, 1921.

———. "Briney Will Be Recommended as Chief of Police." August 14, 1918.

———. "Cambria Houses Above Franklin Being Finished." December 28, 1918.

———. "Cambria Steel Company Announces Resumption of Mill Operations." November 12, 1919.

———. "Cambria Steel Company Installs Sinter Plant in Its Works at Rosedale." September 14, 1921.

———. "Cambria Steel Is Making Progress on Mining Plant." September 17, 1917.

———. "Capt. Fink Reported Very Much Improved." September 27, 1923.

———. "Capt. Fink Submits to Removal of Lead." September 7, 1923.

———. "Catherine Wazniac Attacked by Negro." June 20, 1923.

———. "Cauffiel for Mayor and Entire Republican Ticket Elected to Other Offices." November 5, 1919.

———. "Cauffiel Leads in Mayor Fight by 351 Plurality." November 10, 1927.

———. "Chief Briney Cleared and Restored to Duty; Verdict Is Unanimous." February 28, 1922.

———. "Chief of Police Is Suspended by Orders of Mayor." February 16, 1922.

———. "Churches to Come to Aid of Mayor in His Fight Against Booze" January 1, 1921.

———. "City Council Refunds Fines in Four Cases Appealed from Mayor." January 16, 1923.

———. "City Officials Call on Wounded Officers." September 6, 1923.

———. "City Takes Steps to Stop Possible Race Riots Here." July 31, 1917.

———. "Colored Boys to Dine at Stanwix Before Leaving." October 26, 1917.

———. "Colored Couple United by Alderman Levergood." July 31, 1918.

———. "Colored Draftees Given a Rousing Sendoff Saturday." October 29, 1917.

———. "Colored Draftees of County Zone 1 Will Leave Aug. 3." July 30, 1918.

———. "Colored Men Will Entrain August 3; 39 Are on the List." July 29, 1918.

———. "Colored Soldiers Get Same Sendoff as the White Boys." October 27, 1917.

———. "Conemaugh Negress Seriously Wounded." June 18, 1921.

———. "Conference Opens in Local Church." October 2, 1918.

———. "Corpse Regains Life as Officers Hound 'Murderer.'" December 1, 1922.

———. "Council Defeats $7,500 Bill for Salary of Mayor." July 10, 1923.

———. "Court Directs Verdict for Ex-Mayor Cauffiel." March 20, 1918.

———. "'Craps Game' in Franklin Boro Brings on Fight." May 11, 1923.

———. "Death of County Detective Holds up Prosecutions." September 1, 1923.

———. "Declares There Was a 'Frame-Up' to Get Her." August 2, 1918.

———. "Detective Otto Nukem Succumbs of Heart Attack." September 13, 1923.

———. "Detectives Raid Opium Den Which Is in Full Swing." January 12, 1921.

———. "Diversity of Characters Come before Mayor with a Kelly Talking Slavish." December 2, 1919.

———. "Dr. Clayborne Claims that He Defended Self." January 1, 1919.

———. "'Drive' on the Loafers Resumed." July 26, 1918.

———. "Dr. Palmer Takes Rap at Mayor Cauffiel for Stand on Regularity." October 13, 1922.

———. "Druggist Prosecutes Mayor after Sending an Accuser to Jail." December 31, 1920.

———. "Early Voting Is Very Heavy." November 14, 1919.

———. "Effect an Agreement in Controversy over Relocating Car Lines." May 21, 1921.

———. "Five Suspects Are Arrested in Culin Case." February 19, 1920.

———. "Former Mayor Cauffiel Succumbs to Lingering Illness at His Home." July 10, 1932.

———. "Frameup, Declares Negro, When Wife Recites Her Story." April 9, 1917.

———. "Franklin Borough Is Said to Be Mecca for 'Bad' Negroes." September 21, 1920.

———. "Franklin Man Is Found Murdered in His Bedroom." November 19, 1920.

———. "From Funeral of John Barleycorn to Mayor's Court." July 1, 1919.

———. "Garbage Injunction Case Is Heard Today by Judge J.A. Berkey." August 26, 1921.

———. "Gave Herself to Police after She Had Cut a Woman." August 26, 1918.

———. "George Mills to Face Charge for Shooting Negro." May 15, 1922.

———. "Governor Wants Facts of Order." September 19, 1923.

———. "Head of Charities Body Tells about Migration of Negro in Pennsylvania" October 19, 1917.

———. "He's Not the Man." September 27, 1904.

———. "Hold Colored Man on Murder Charge." November 12, 1921.

———. "Hon. J.W. Johnson Will Speak Here." April 11, 1918.

———. "Hunger Keeps Mexican Army Ranks Filled." June 17, 1916.

———. "Importation of Negroes Opposed." August 2, 1919.

———. "Injunctions Against Liquor Men Continued Following Arguments." February 19, 1921.

———. "Johnstown Police Kept Busy During Month of February." March 2, 1917.

———. "Joseph Cauffiel Enters a Plea of Guilty in Court." March 16, 1921.

———. "Joseph Cauffiel Named Defendant in Suit Recorded." July 26, 1917.

———. "Ku Klux Klan Burns Crosses Last Night." September 8, 1923.

———. "Ku Klux Klan Holds Ceremonial." August 25, 1922.

———. "Larger City Jail and More Policemen Recommended by Chief Swabb in Report." February 12, 1918.

———. "Law and Order." September 2, 1923.

———. "Lieut. Otto Fink Elected Captain of Police Force." February 13, 1923.

———. "Mayor Brings an Officer to Task." February 22, 1922.

———. "Mayor Calls for Warrant When Landlord of Labor Temple Fails to Appear." January 19, 1920.

———. "Mayor Calls 100 Men to Help Him Enforce Volstead Act Locally." August 14, 1922.

———. "Mayor Carries Threat to Close Restaurants." January 1, 1923.

———. "Mayor Cauffiel Closes Three Local Hotels in Surprise Night Visits." August 2, 1922.

————. "Mayor Cauffiel in Annual Message." January 2, 1923.

————. "Mayor Cauffiel Issues Permit to Dr. Palmer for His Mass Meeting." October 23, 1922.

————. "Mayor Cauffiel Opens War on Violators of Prohibition Statutes." September 12, 1921.

————. "Mayor Cauffiel Turns His Executive Wrath on Group of Men and Women." January 8, 1923.

————. "Mayor Cauffiel Would Fix Salary of His Office at $7,500 per Annum." July 3, 1923.

————. "Mayor Denounces Agents Who Send in Undesirables." January 17, 1923.

————. "Mayor Grants Permission to Hotelmen." August 19, 1922.

————. "Mayor Has Tilt with Council Over Paying Salary of Policeman." January 17, 1922.

————. "Mayor Invokes Police Powers to Stop Work of Relocating Tracks." May 19, 1921.

————. "Mayor Liberates Most of Inmates at Local Prison." March 30, 1923.

————. "Mayor Loses Three of His 'Sleuths" in One Day; All Down on Job." January 5, 1921.

————. "Mayor Orders the Arrest of Loafers on City's Streets." March 1, 1918.

————. "Mayor May Stand Trial for Alleged Shooting at Negro." March 31, 1921.

————. "Mayor Refuses a Permit to Circus." April 4, 1918.

————. "Mayor Refuses Dr. Palmer a Permit for His Meeting." October 21, 1922.

————. "Mayor Rests Crusade to Watch Actions of Federal Operatives." August 21, 1922.

————. "Mayor Says Labor Hall Is Nuisance; Orders It Abated." January 10, 1920.

————. "Mayor Says Vice Crusade Is On; Chief Says 'No.'" November 23, 1920.

————. "Mayor's Case Is Delayed and Mob Is Disappointed." January 6, 1921.

————. "Mayor's Charges Against Briney Given an Airing." February 22, 1922.

————. "Mayor Sentenced to Pay $500 Fine, 60 Days in Jail." December 20, 1921.

———. "Mayor's Police Court Prisoners All Discharged." January 7, 1924.

———. "Mayor Suspends Chief of Police; Later Reinstated." February 14, 1922.

———. "Mayor Tells Man He Needs Beating Instead of Fine." October 4, 1920.

———. "Mayor Uses Police Power to Close Up Bars of Defendants." December 29, 1920.

———. "Mayor Visits Hill District." March 4, 1919.

———. "Memorial Places Conveniences at Officers' Demand." September 1, 1923.

———. "Mexican Accused of Minersville Gunplay Caught." September 5, 1922.

———. "Mexican Alleged to Have Attacked Girls Fined $100." January 28, 1918.

———. "Mexican Facing Serious Charges Following Fight." April 2, 1917.

———. "Mexican Laborer Found Dead Near Cambria Oredump." July 5, 1922.

———. "Mob Chases Negro in Franklin Plant." September 11, 1923.

———. "Moose Donate to Policeman's Fund." September 18, 1923.

———. "More Police for Outlying Sections." February 13, 1919.

———. "More than $1,300 Added to Officers' Fund from Circus." September 20, 1923.

———. "Negress Badly Cut in Jealousy Fight." February 5, 1923.

———. "Negro Accused of Attack upon girl." November 7, 1921.

———. "Negro Arrested." September 26, 1904.

———. "Negro Arrested Connected with Robbery Affair." April 6, 1921.

———. "Negro Arrested for Pittsburgh on Charge of Murder." February 22, 1917.

———. "Negro Arrested in Holdup Affair." December 4, 1922.

———. "Negro Badly Cut during Fight in Rosedale House." April 22, 1921.

———. "Negro Chauffeur Is Held for Violation." April 7, 1922.

———. "Negro Confesses to His Part in Brutal Assault." October 13, 1920.

———. "Negro Divulges Secret Process of Wine-Making." July 28, 1919.

———. "Negro Doorkeeper Is Sent to Jail." August 18, 1920.

———. "Negro Educator Tells of Fight for Race Rights." December 6, 1919.

———. "Negroes Brutally Attack and Rob a Haynes Street Shoemaker; One Is Caught." August 2, 1920.

———. "Negroes Object to Sign Reading 'For Whites Only.'" February 22, 1923.

————. "Negro Gets Heavy Fine for Insults." September 12, 1922.

————. "Negro Held for Attack on Youth." April 4, 1921.

————. "Negro Hits Woman with Ax; 'I Loved Her,' Tells Police." March 26, 1919.

————. "Negro Introduces Entirely New Way of Getting Drunk." January 31, 1923.

————. "Negro Is Given Fine; Appeal Will Be Taken." July 6, 1923.

————. "Negro May Be Brought Here." September 29, 1904.

————. "Negro Order Is Refused Right to Solicit Here." September 24, 1918.

————. "Negro Pines for Old 'Wet' Times." July 24, 1919.

————. "Negro Shoots Self after He Murders Wife." January 30, 1919.

————. "Negro Slays Wife with Ax." May 22, 1920.

————. "Negro Suspected of Theft Faces Larceny Charge." March 20, 2017.

————. "Negro Who Shot Woman Had a Big Cartridge Supply." February 10, 1919.

————. "Negro Workman Shot to Death in a Quarrel at Nathan Operations." April 10, 1922.

————. "New Figures of Justice in Police Court Room." November 21, 1917.

————. "New Mayor and City Councilmen Take Oaths of Office and Assume…" January 5, 1920.

————. "New Mayor Holds Court; Appoints New Interpreter." January 6, 1916.

————. "New Record Is Set by Federal-State Employment Bureau." April 16, 1918.

————. "No Change Reported as Officers Grimly Battle in Hospitals." September 1, 1923.

————. "Officer Gets Word from the War Zone." March 13, 2017.

————. "Officer Shot to Save Self." December 4, 1918.

————. "One Policeman Dead, Another Probably Fatally Wounded, Victims of Franklin Negro's Deadly Aim; Resisting Arrest." September 21, 1927.

————. "Ordered Mexicans off the Sidewalk." January 13, 1917.

————. "Orders Negroes to Leave Johnstown." September 4, 1923.

————. "Oversight of Mayor Causes Continuance of 'Tippling' Cases." August 15, 1922.

————. "Pleads for Life While Two Negroes Rob Him." July 31, 1920.

———. "Pleads, 'Private Stock,' as Cause of Beautiful Jag." May 28, 1920.

———. "Plea for Funds for Boy Scouts Made to Rotary." April 19, 1922.

———. "The Police." September 1, 1923.

———. "Police Are Combing Hills to Capture a Negro for Shooting." April 13, 1917.

———. "Police Aroused by Reported Attacks on Women in City." January 25, 1918.

———. "Police Believe Two Assailants in Murder Case." July 7, 1922.

———. "Police Break in on Poker Party." December 26, 1919.

———. "Police Court Is Tame with Booze Cases Wiped Out." January 22, 1920.

———. "Police Fund Has Reached $7,300." September 22, 1923.

———. "Police Hunting Negro Suspected of Cutting Nash." February 5, 1917.

———. "Policeman Kills Negro Following Fight at Franklin." December 3, 1918.

———. "Policeman Shot by Negro Is in Critical State." November 13, 1918.

———. "Policeman Virgin Again Figures in Exciting Arrest." January 20, 1923.

———. "Police Officers Given a Hearing by City Council." January 30, 1922.

———. "Police Officers Improve Slightly, Reports Indicate." September 4, 1923.

———. "Police Officials Not Anticipating Any Disturbance." August 6, 1917.

———. "Police Records Heaviest in the History of City." July 3, 1918.

———. "Police Round Up Many Suspicious Persons in City." May 9, 1921.

———. "Police Suspect 'Frame-Up' and Negro Is Freed." May 2, 1918.

———. "Poolrooms Must Close at 1 a.m., Says Chief Swabb." March 8, 1918.

———. "Presbyterian Pastor Deplores Defiance of Laws and Authority." September 10, 1923.

———. "The Primaries." September 17, 1923.

———. "Prison's Menu Is Costing Too Much; 'Guests Must Pay.'" May 25, 1918.

———. "Protest against *The Klansman*." November 10, 1906.

———. "Quota Club Will Aid Officers' Fund." September 5, 1923.

———. "Race Distinctions and Religious Differences Have No Place in War." May 11, 1918.

————. "Refuse New Trial in Case against Joseph Cauffiel." June 2, 1921.

————. "Regular Drilling for Policemen Is Proposed by Chief." April 9, 1918.

————. "Rosedale." September 1, 1923.

————. "Rosedale Annex Goes to Council." February 12, 1918.

————. "Rosedale Council Passes Finally Ordinance Asking Admission to Greater City." December 14, 1917.

————. "Rosedale Negro Dies of Gunshot Wounds in Fight." November 10, 1921.

————. "Rosedale Will Be Part of the City Friday Morning." June 19, 1918.

————. "Rumor that Election of Mr. Cauffiel to Be Contested Caused Stir." November 27, 1919.

————. "Sacred Concert for Police Relief Fund." September 6, 1923.

————. "Selling Whiskey Is Same as Bartering in Humans—Mayor." December 16, 1920.

————. "Special Meetings Soon for Rosedale." July 12, 1923.

————. "Spectacular Contests Mark Primary." September 19, 1923.

————. "State Continues Investigation of Alleged 'Order.'" September 24, 1923.

————. "Story of Struggle in Darkness Told by Two Policemen." August 31, 1923.

————. "Strange Mixture of Men Assemble before the Mayor." May 24, 1920.

————. "Thefts of Suits Get Two Negroes into Police Court." January 26, 1923.

————. "Three Arrested in a Pool Room Fight." February 7, 1917.

————. "Three Arrests in Theft at Rosedale." August 20, 1923.

————. "Three Colored People Taken in Police Raid." January 21, 1922.

————. "Three Dead, Two More Wounded in Rosedale Shooting; County Detective James One of Victims." August 31, 1923.

————. "Three Mexicans Apprehended for Carrying Knives." December 19, 1921.

————. "Thrown Off Clue." September 23, 1904.

————. "Trying Doors; Two Arrested." August 22, 1918.

————. "Two Alleged Chicken Thieves Arrested in Rosedale House Raid." March 8, 1922.

————. "Two Colored Men Shot in Rosedale Bunkhouse Fight." August 15, 1923.

————. "Two Detectives Are Demoted by Mayor Cauffiel." January 16, 1922.

———. "Undesirable Publicity." September 22, 1923.

———. "Victim of Shooting Dies; Negro Facing Charge of Murder." April 14, 1917.

———. "Wage Increase for the Policemen Impossible Now, Is the Decision." July 11, 1918.

———. "Wants Reward of $1,000 or More Offered." February 21, 1920.

———. "Wave of Crime on 'The Hill.'" February 24, 1919.

———. "Week-End Arrests Fill Up Central Police Station." September 3, 1923.

———. "Week-End Proved Busy for Police; Have Many Calls." May 28, 1923.

———. "Work on Cambria Plate Mill Stops." July 19, 1917.

———. "Year in Jail Is before Him Who Carries a Flask." January 16, 1920.

———. "Y.M.C.A. Organized for Colored Men." January 18, 1919.

Johnstown (PA) Tribune-Democrat. Special section on "Black History." February 12, 1980.

Jones, Bill. "Learning from the Past." *Johnstown Tribune-Democrat*, September 13, 1998.

Journal News. "'Moon' Crazed Negro Kills 2, 3 Others Dying." August 31, 1923.

Kane (PA) Republican. "'Advised' Negroes to Leave Says Johnstown Mayor." September 20, 1923.

———. "Hurls Defiance at Critics." September 19, 1923.

———. "Verdict Against Johnstown Mayor." March 16, 1922.

Kansas City (KS) Advocate. "Mayor Joseph Cauffiel." October 19, 1923.

Lebanon (PA) Daily News. "Negroes Remain in Johnstown." September 15, 1923.

Lemann, Nicholas. *The Promised Land: The Great Black Migration and How It Changed America.* New York: Vintage Books, 1992.

Lewis, Ira. Letter from Ira Lewis to Gifford Pinchot. From Gifford Pinchot Papers, Box 1499, Manuscripts Division, Library of Congress.

Lincoln County News. "Over 2,000 Negroes Depart…" September 17, 1923.

Literary Digest. "Johnstown's Flood of Negro Labor." October 6, 1923.

Loewen, James W. *Sundown Towns: A Hidden Dimension of American Racism.* New York: Touchstone Books, 2005.

Los Angeles Times. "Is This America?" October 3, 1923.

Loucks, Emerson. *The Ku Klux Klan in Pennsylvania.* Harrisburg, PA: Telegraph Press, 1936.

Macfarland Chas S. Letter from Chas S. Macfarland to Gov. Gifford Pinchot. From Gifford Pinchot Papers, Box 1499, Manuscripts Division, Library of Congress.

Mandall, Melissa. "La Prensa and the Mexican Workers of Bethlehem Steel." *Pennsylvania Legacies* (November 2006).

Manser, James D. Letter from James D. Manser to Gifford Pinchot. From Gifford Pinchot Papers, Box 1499, Manuscripts Division, Library of Congress.

Marshall (TX) Messenger. "Another Train of Mexicans Moves East." July 11, 1923.

Marshall (TX) News Messenger. "Council Churches Says Klan a Menace." December 16, 1923.

———. "Mexican Embassy Asks Report on Johnstown Case." September 20, 1923.

———. "The Negro Up North." September 21, 1923.

McDevitt, Cody. "Oldest Black Church in Johnstown Led the Way on Civil Rights." *Daily American*, September 7, 2017.

McGeary, M. Nelson. *Gifford Pinchot: Forester-Politician*. Princeton, NJ: Princeton University Press, 1960.

Messenger and Intelligencer. "Not Hospitable to Blacks." September 20, 1923.

Michaeli, Ethan. *The Defender: How the Legendary Black Newspaper Changed America*. Boston: Houghton Mifflin Harcourt, 2016.

Minneapolis (MN) Star. "Go Back South." January 21, 1924.

Monroe Journal (Monroeville, AL). "Mayor Will Drive Negroes from City." September 18, 1923.

Moore, Lewis B. Letter from Lewis B. Moore to Gifford Pinchot. From Gifford Pinchot Papers, Box 1499, Manuscripts Division, Library of Congress.

Morning Call. "Johnstown Puts Mayor Cauffiel in His Place." September 23, 1923.

Morning Herald. "Cauffiel Orders Negroes from Johnstown." September 15, 1923.

Morning News. "Movement of Colored People." September 26, 1923.

Morning Register. "Official Law-Breaking." September 29, 1923.

Muncie (IN) Evening Press. "What Would an Alien Think?" September 20, 1923.

"N.A.A.C.P. Acts on Wholesale Deportation of Negroes." September 20, 1923, Pg 1. Accessed April 26, 2017, newspapers.com.

National Association for the Advancement of Colored People Records, 1919–1991. Library of Congress. Manuscripts Division.

New Castle (PA) Herald. "As We See It." September 19, 1923.

———. "Short of Police in Johnstown, PA." May 15, 1923.

New Castle (PA) News. "Probe in Johnstown of Negro Expulsion Is Closed." September 24, 1923.

News-Herald. "3 Killed, Same Number Injured in Negro Riot." August 31, 1923.

News Journal. "Johnstown's Mayor." September 20, 1923.

News Leader. "Negroes Up North." September 19, 1923.

New York Age. "Comments by the Age Editors on Sayings of Other Editors." October 13, 1923.

———. "Is This Within the Law?" September 22, 1923.

———. "Negroes Ordered to Leave Johnstown by Mayor Joseph Cauffiel." September 22, 1923.

New York Amsterdam News. "The Cradle Is Rocking." September 19, 1923.

———. "Johnstown Mayor Attempts to Carry Out Drastic Order that Negro Residents Must Leave." September 19, 1923.

New York Times. "Johnstown Expels 2,000 Workingmen." September 14, 1923.

Ogden (UT) Standard-Examiner. "Rum Crazed Negro Kills 2, Wounds 3." August 31, 1923.

Orlando (FL) Sentinel. "Johnstown's Mayor Says He Did Not Ban Negroes." September 20, 1923.

Owens, Chandler. "The Russian Czar of Johnstown." *Pittsburgh Courier,* September 15, 1923.

Owens, John. W. "Johnstown Trouble Laid to 'Set-up' Negro." *Baltimore Sun,* September 27, 1923.

Owensboro (KY) Messenger. "Face Prejudice." September 20, 1923.

Palm Beach (FL) Post. "No Formal Order; Advised to Leave." September 20, 1923.

———. "State to Act to Protect Negroes." September 19, 1923.

Peabody, George Foster. Letter from George Foster Peabody to Gifford Pinchot. From Gifford Pinchot Papers, Box 1499, Manuscripts Division, Library of Congress.

Peets, T.D. Letter from T.D. Peets to Gifford Pinchot. From Gifford Pinchot Papers, Box 1499, Manuscripts Division, Library of Congress.

Pesqueira, F.A. Letter from F.A. Pesqueira to Gifford Pinchot. From Gifford Pinchot Papers, Box 1499, Manuscripts Division, Library of Congress.

Philadelphia Inquirer. "Boston Negroes Protest to Coolidge and Pinchot." September 20, 1923.

———. "Boy Victim of Riot Says Hooded Crowd Beat Warned Man." June 12, 1924.

————. "Cambria G.O.P. in Militant Mood." November 6, 1927.

————. "Johnstown Ejects Negroes after Riot." September 15, 1923.

————. "Many Court Evils Found by Probers." August 8, 1938.

————. "Old Cambria Feud Breaks Out Again." April 3, 1927.

————. "Ruth Report Urges 10 Steps to Fight Crime, Grand Juries Praised." August 8, 1938.

————. "25 Negroes Ordered out of Johnstown." December 5, 1923.

Philadelphia Tribune. Letter from *Philadelphia Tribune* to Gifford Pinchot. From Gifford Pinchot Papers, Box 1499, Manuscripts Division, Library of Congress.

Phillips, William. Letter from William Phillips to Gifford Pinchot. From Gifford Pinchot Papers, Box 1499, Manuscripts Division, Library of Congress.

Pickens, William. Letter from William Pickens to Gifford Pinchot. From Gifford Pinchot Papers, Box 1499, Manuscripts Division, Library of Congress.

Pinchot, Gifford. Letter from Gifford Pinchot to Dr. Hinkson. From Gifford Pinchot Papers, Box 1499, Manuscripts Division, Library of Congress.

————. Letter from Gifford Pinchot to F.A. Pesqueira. From Gifford Pinchot Papers, Box 1499, Manuscripts Division, Library of Congress.

————. Letter from Gifford Pinchot to James Weldon Johnson. From Gifford Pinchot Papers, Box 1499, Manuscripts Division, Library of Congress.

————. Letter from Gifford Pinchot to Mayor Joseph Cauffiel. From Gifford Pinchot Papers, Box 1499, Manuscripts Division, Library of Congress.

————. Letter from Gifford Pinchot to Mrs. Joseph M. Gazzam. From Gifford Pinchot Papers, Box 1499, Manuscripts Division, Library of Congress.

————. Letter from Gifford Pinchot to J. Silas Harris. From Gifford Pinchot Papers, Box 1499, Manuscripts Division, Library of Congress.

————. Letter from Gifford Pinchot to Lewis B. Moore. From Gifford Pinchot Papers, Box 1499, Manuscripts Division, Library of Congress.

————. Letter from Gifford Pinchot to L. Hollingsworth Wood. From Gifford Pinchot Papers, Box 1499, Manuscripts Division, Library of Congress.

————. Letter from Gifford Pinchot to Lynn G. Adams. From Gifford Pinchot Papers, Box 1499, Manuscripts Division, Library of Congress.

————. Letter from Gifford Pinchot to Rev. Robert B. St. Clair. From Gifford Pinchot Papers, Box 1499, Manuscripts Division, Library of Congress.

———. Letter from Gifford Pinchot to R.R. Wright. From Gifford Pinchot Papers, Box 1499, Manuscripts Division, Library of Congress.

———. Letter from Gifford Pinchot to William Phillips. From Gifford Pinchot Papers, Box 1499, Manuscripts Division, Library of Congress.

Pittsburgh Courier. "Citizens of Johnstown Reply to Order by Defeating him at Polls." September 22, 1923.

———. "Defeated at Polls and Attacked on All Sides Cauffiel 'Crawfishes.'" September 29, 1923.

———. "Dr. Burrell K. Johnson." April 1, 1933.

———. "Editorial Comment on White Press of Walton-Cauffiel 'Law and Order' Edict." September 29, 1923.

———. "Johnstown Offers South Propaganda." September 29, 1923.

———. "Johnstown Repudiates Mayor." September 22, 1923.

———. "Johnstown Unfair to Negroes." August 24, 1957.

———. "Labor Pledges Aid in Defense of Race Worker." November 24, 1923.

———. "Mexico Protests Johnstown Order Against Nationals." September 20, 1923.

———. "Nevermore Cauffiel." October 13, 1923.

———. "Page President Wannamaker." October 6, 1923.

———. "Southern White Journal Comes to Our Defense." November 24, 1923.

Pittsburgh Daily Post. "Cambria Mob Seeks a Life: Hundreds of Excited Men Gather at Patton to Seize Negro Suspect." September 23, 1904.

———. "Cauffiel Reiterates Order to Negroes to Get Out of Johnstown." September 19, 1923.

———. "Johnstown Negro Kills Two Officers." September 1, 1923.

———. "Jury Finds $10,000 Verdict Against Johnstown Mayor." October 20, 1923.

———. "Marcus Garvey Talks to 2,000 in Tabernacle." October 2, 1923.

———. "Negro Admits Murder." May 23, 1920.

———. "Old Woman Slain Near Johnstown." February 18, 1920.

———. "Police Chief Kills Negro." December 4, 1918.

———. "Police Relief Fund." September 23, 1923.

Pittsburgh Post-Gazette. "Cauffiel 'Order' Is Now Request." September 20, 1923.

———. "Society's Higher Duty." October 11, 1923.

Pittsburgh Press. "Additional Society." June 27, 1920.

———. "Funeral of Slain Police Captain Held." November 6, 1923.

———. "Johnstown Riot Area Guard Is Strengthened." September 1, 1923.

———. "Johnstown's Booze Hoax Is Publicity." *Pittsburgh Press*, August 21, 1922.

———. "Mills Outlook Reported Good in Johnstown." October 14, 1923.

———. "Mob Seeks the Life of Negro." September 23, 1904.

———. "Probe of Johnstown Expulsion Brought to Close by State." September 24, 1923.

———. "Probe Ordered into Cauffiel's Alleged Action." September 23, 1923.

———. "Sale of Firearms Banned in Johnstown by Mayor." September 2, 1923.

———. "Three Killed, Four Injured in Riot at Johnstown." August 31, 1923.

Portsmouth (NH) Herald. "Three Killed in Race Riot." August 31, 1923.

Press and Sun-Bulletin. "Mayor Insists Negroes Leave." September 20, 1923.

———. "Throwing Refuse into Your Neighbor's Yard." September 18, 1923.

Press-Forum Weekly. "Gov. Pinchot Guarantees Negroes' Rights." September 29, 1923.

———. "Southern Editors on Race Relations." November 3, 1923.

Reading (PA) Times. "Defies Pinchot." September 19, 1923.

Reidsville (NC) Review. "President Obregon." September 21, 1923.

Reno (NV) Gazette-Journal. "Not 'Deported;' Advised to Go." September 20, 1923.

Report on the Steel Strike of 1919. New York: Harcourt, Brace and Howe, 1920.

Republic. "The Johnstown Tragedy." September 6, 1923.

Rockford (AL) Chronicle. "'Promised Land' Is Now Becoming Unpromising." November 8, 1923.

Roger William Riis Papers. ACLU Reel. Library of Congress. Manuscripts Division.

Rutledge, Eleanor Cauffiel. "Joseph Cauffiel Tribute for the Barefoot Reunion Association Booklet." Accessed May 1, 2019, www.familysearch. org/service/records/storage/das-mem/patron/v2/TH-904-56898-483-1/dist.txt?ctx=ArtCtxPublic.

San Francisco Examiner. "Wants Clergyman to Be the Chief of Police." December 17, 1911.

Schrag, Peter. *Not Fit for Our Society: Immigration and Nativism in America*. Berkeley: University of California Press, 2010.

Scranton (PA) Republican. "Johnstown Mayor Explains Actions." September 20, 1923.

Sherman, Richard B. "Johnstown v. the Negro: Southern Migrants and the Exodus of 1923." *Pennsylvania History: A Journal of Mid-Atlantic Studies.* University Park, PA: Penn State University Press, 1963.

Simmons, Roscoe. "The Week." *Chicago Defender*, October 6, 1923.

———. "The Week." *Chicago Defender*, September 29, 1923.

———. "The Week." *Chicago Defender*, September 22, 1923.

Simpson County News (Mendenhall, MS). "Arkansas Negro, Back from North, Advises Others Stay Here." November 15, 1923.

Somerset (PA) Herald. "Negro Settlement Closely Guarded." September 1, 1923.

Star Progress. "The Mayor of Johnstown." September 21, 1923.

Star Tribune. "How Blacks Live in Johnstown, Pa." October 4, 1923.

———. "Mockeries on Constitution Day." September 19, 1923.

———. "The Mote and the Beam." September 28, 1923.

St. Clair, Robert B. Letter from Robert B. St. Clair to Gifford Pinchot. From Gifford Pinchot Papers, Box 1499, Manuscripts Division, Library of Congress.

St. Louis (MO) Post-Dispatch. "Race Problem in Johnstown." September 17, 1923.

St. Louis (MO) Star and Times. "The President's Contradictions." December 7, 1923.

———. "Reaction Against Negro Immigrants." September 14, 1923.

———. "South Carolina Lectures Pennsylvania." September 18, 1923.

Sullivan, Patricia. *Lift Every Voice: The NAACP and the Making of the Civil Rights Movement.* New York: New Press, 2009.

Tampa (FL) Times. "The Negro." September 28, 1923.

Tatum, Elbert Lee. *Changed Political Thought of the Negro: 1915–1940.* Westport, CT: Greenwood Press, 1974.

Taylor (TX) Daily Press. "Expulsion of Mexican Is Under Attack." September 22, 1923.

Times. "Exiled Mexicans Will Be Allowed to Return." September 22, 1923.

Times Herald. "Wire Briefs." September 20, 1923.

Titusville (PA) Herald. "Negroes Only Advised to Leave." September 20, 1923.

Tribune. "Johnstown Voters Prove Americanism." September 25, 1923.

Unknown author. Letter from unknown author to Mrs. Louise H. Burrell. NAACP Papers, Library of Congress, Roll C138.

Vargas, Zaragosa. "Armies in the Fields and Factories: The Mexican Working Classes in the Midwest in the 1920s." *Mexican Studies/Estudios Mexicanos* 7, no. 1 (Winter 1991): 47–71.

Walker, Samuel. *In Defense of American Liberties: A History of the ACLU.* Oxford: Oxford University Press, 1990.

Wannamaker, J.S. Letter from J.S. Wannamaker to Gifford Pinchot. From Gifford Pinchot Papers, Box 1499, Manuscripts Division, Library of Congress.

———. Telegram from J.S. Wannamaker to Gifford Pinchot. From Gifford Pinchot Papers, Box 1499, Manuscripts Division, Library of Congress.

Ward, Cassius. Letter from Cassius Ward to Gifford Pinchot. From Gifford Pinchot Papers, Box 1499, Manuscripts Division, Library of Congress.

Washburn, Patrick S. *The African American Newspaper: Voice of Freedom.* Evanston, IL: Northwestern University Press, 2006.

Watchman and Southron (Sumter, SC). "Cotton Fight Is Sound and Right." April 5, 1919.

White, Walter. Letter from Walter F. White to Frank Steward. NAACP Papers, Library of Congress, Roll C138.

Whittle, Randy. *Johnstown, Pennsylvania: A History, Part 1.* Charleston, SC: The History Press, 2005.

———. *Johnstown, Pennsylvania: A History, Part 2.* Charleston, SC: The History Press, 2007.

Wilkerson, Isabel. *The Warmth of Other Suns.* New York: Vintage Books, 2010.

Wilkes-Barre (PA) Times-Leader. "Negro Murdered." December 16, 1922.

———. "Three Men Slain in Johnstown Riot." September 1, 1923.

Williams, Bruce T. *We'll Take the Journey: The African-American Story of Johnstown, Migration and Work.* Directed by Bruce T. Williams. Johnstown, Pennsylvania, 1992.

Williams, Marco. *Banished.* Directed by Marco Williams. San Francisco, 2007.

Wilson, Rose. Letter from Rose Wilson to Gifford Pinchot. From Gifford Pinchot Papers, Box 1499, Manuscripts Division, Library of Congress.

Wilson, Sondra K. *The Selected Writings of James Weldon Johnson.* New York: Oxford University Press, 1995.

Winston County Signal (Louisville, MS). "Drastic Order Against Negroes." September 20, 1923.

Wood, L. Hollingsworth. Letter from L. Hollingsworth Wood to Gifford Pinchot. From Gifford Pinchot Papers, Box 1499, Manuscripts Division, Library of Congress.

Woodruff, George. Letter from George W. Woodruff to James Weldon Johnson. From Gifford Pinchot Papers, Box 1499, Manuscripts Division, Library of Congress.

Woodson, Carter. *A Century of Negro Migration: The Exodus.* Scotts Valley, CA: CreateSpace Independent Publishing Platform, 2014.

Woofter, Thomas Jackson, Jr. *Negro Migration: Changes in Rural Organization and Population of the Cotton Belt*. London: Forgotten Books, 2015.

Wright. R.R. Letter from R.R. Wright to Gifford Pinchot. From Gifford Pinchot Papers, Box 1499, Manuscripts Division, Library of Congress.

Zolberg, Aristide R. *A Nation by Design: Immigration Police in the Fashioning of America*. Cambridge, MA: Harvard University Press, 2006.

ABOUT THE AUTHOR

Cody McDevitt is an award-winning journalist and the founder of the Rosedale Oral History Project, which is the basis for *Banished from Johnstown: Racist Backlash in Pennsylvania.* Recently, he released a compendium of firsthand accounts of veterans who fought in World War II called *Answering the Call: Somerset County during World War II.* He is also the coauthor of *Pittsburgh Drinks: A History of Cocktails, Nightlife & Bartending Tradition,* which is available on Amazon and in select bookstores locally. He lives near Pittsburgh and works for the *Somerset Daily American.*